INTERPRETATION OF THE 1961 ILLINOIS TEST OF PSYCHOLINGUISTIC ABILITIES

WITH REPRODUCTIONS OF ORIGINAL PROFILES

Barbara D. Bateman

University of Oregon

Published and Distributed by **SPECIAL CHILD PUBLICATIONS**

Seattle, Washington

Printed in the United States of America

This interpretation is applicable to both the experimental and new revised edition of the ITPA.

PREFACE AND ACKNOWLEDGEMENTS

The Illinois Test of Psycholinguistic Abilities (ITPA) is now in use in schools, clinics, research projects, and university training programs throughout the country. The widespread use and acceptance of this new instrument while it was still in the Experimental edition (1961) attests to the reality and the urgency of the needs it was designed to meet. Many of those using or contemplating using the test have expressed a desire for information beyond that in the test manual to aid in interpreting profiles. The purpose of this monograph is to share with the reader the clinical observations and data accumulated during several years' use of the ITPA. It should be emphasized that these are only the observations and opinions of one clinician and that research findings as such have been presented elsewhere (Bateman, 1965 and Appendix--Bibliography of ITPA Literature, 1960-1967).

The reader should also note that the ITPA is being revised and that this monograph presents observations and profiles based on the 1961 Experimental edition of the test. However, the principles of interpretation are believed to be directly applicable to both editions of the test and many of the specific observations will perhaps be applicable with only minor or readily apparent modifications.

To the authors of the ITPA, Drs. Samuel A. Kirk and James J. McCarthy, go the thanks of the writer and all those who have used the test for their invaluable contribution to diagnosing and alleviating psycholinguistic disabilities. And to the scores of students and staff of the Institute for Research on Exceptional Children, University of Illinois, who for the past several years have studied, used, criticized, and refined the test and its applications, gratitude is expressed. Without them, the observations in this paper could not have been made.

And to Sr. Joanne Marie Kliebhan, Ph.D., whose support, encouragement, and extensive and able assistance are responsible for these observations being in written form, deepest gratitude is acknowledged.

The author also expresses sincere thanks to Mrs. Shirley Olson who typed the manuscript.

CONTENTS

FOREWORD

Children with learning problems are not discoveries of the Jet Age. Such children probably baffled the teacher in the one-room schoolhouse of grandmother's time as much as they do the teachers in modern nursery schools and ungraded primary classes. But there is increasing interest in the subject and increasing focus on what can be done to ameliorate the condition. The learning-disabled child was formerly considered generally backward or dull and deemed incapable of regular education. Today the emphasis is on early detection and differential diagnosis of learning disorders is an attempt to prevent and remediate specific areas of disability.

Among the influential factors that have contributed to the current interest in diagnosis and remediation of learning problems was the publication in 1961 of the Illinois Test of Psycholinguistic Abilities (ITPA). While still in the experimental edition, the ITPA has received wide acclaim as a useful screening instrument in the discovery of psycholinguistic disabilities and as an aid in remedial planning. The test has been in extensive use in schools, clinics, and research projects throughout this country and abroad.

Of the many users of the ITPA, none appears more qualified to publish a clinical interpretation of the test than Dr. Barbara Bateman. Her several years of work with the ITPA have included early remedial planning, research, clinical usage, educator and psychologist training programs, as well as workshops and seminars throughout the United States. She has compiled in two manuscripts summaries of available research studies in which the Illinois Test of Psycholinguistic Abilities has been used.

Dr. Bateman's TWO YEARS AFTER THE MANUAL was an invaluable aid to the graduate students at the University of Illinois who were fortunate enough to procure copies. Many of the helpful suggestions regarding administration and interpretation included in the original manuscript have been expanded and incorporated in this publication.

INTERPRETATION OF THE 1961 ILLINOIS TEST OF PSYCHOLINGUISTIC ABILITIES promises to be a boon to those psychologists and educators contemplating the use of the ITPA for the first time, as well as to those current users of the test who are seeking specific guidelines for more efficient administration and interpretation.

Sister Joanne Marie Kliebhan, Ph.D.
Cardinal Stritch College
Milwaukee, Wisconsin

CHAPTER 1

PRELIMINARY CONSIDERATIONS

Once any psychological instrument has been administered, the immediate question asked is "what does it mean?" Since the ITPA was especially designed to provide information about the remedial procedures which should be used with the child whose difficulties are being diagnosed, the question often takes the form of "what does this profile tell us about the nature of his educational needs? What are his specific disabilities?"

But before one can begin to discuss the interpretation of a profile one must consider certain prerequisites to that interpretation. This chapter reviews in some detail each of the nine subtests which constitute the profile and presents certain basic prerequisites to their interpretation.

THE ITPA SUBTESTS

An obviously basic prerequisite to profile interpretation is that each of the nine subtest scores on the profile was obtained properly. In other words, each subtest must have been administered, scored, and recorded correctly. Important administration and scoring considerations for each subtest are presented below with additional observations and answers to the questions most frequently asked regarding each.

Auditory - Vocal Automatic
This test measures the subject's ability to use grammatical structures which he has presumably heard in the language spoken in his environment. Grammar is learned "automatically," rather than by reasoned associations. Diagnostically, this subtest indicates the extent to which a child has successfully picked up the linguistic redundancies to which he has been exposed. It may be related to what has been called incidental verbal learning.

HINTS FOR ADMINISTRATION AND SCORING' Examiners often find two major sources of difficulty in this subtest:

(1) On the demonstration item the examiner says, "Here is a bed, Here are two ________." But the subject frequently fails to respond "beds." He often says nothing, says "yes," or says "that makes three." At this point, the examiner may say: "Here is a bed, Here are two ***what***?" In such cases the examiner may also add a second demonstration item utilizing his own fingers. Instructions would then be (with proper gestures): "Here is a finger. Here are two ________." If necessary, the word "what" may again be introduced.

(2) Failure to question all verb items to which an incorrect response is given is also a common fault. ***Any*** incorrect response on a verb item, regardless of the kind of error made, is to be questioned. The questioning techniques outlined in the test manual should be used.

QUESTIONS OFTEN ASKED ABOUT THE SUBTEST. Two questions are often asked about the subtest:

(1) What is the justification for having this test at the non-representational or automatic-sequential level? While it is true that grammatical usage as measured by this test contains a high semantic component, nevertheless, placement at the automatic-sequential level is justified on the grounds that such grammatical usage is acquired automatically or on a habit basis. Few adults can give a reasoned or representational level explanation for the fact, e.g., that when we wish to indicate the past tense of certain verbs such as "stop" and "wreck," we add a final /t/. Although they cannot offer a representational level kind of explanation, they nevertheless have acquired such usage. If, in the future development of the ITPA, the present distinction between the representational and automatic-sequential levels were to be changed and replaced by a distinction drawn according to whether the ability involved was dependent on exposure to a ***particular language***, then the auditory-vocal automatic subtest would probably be moved from the automatic-sequential (non-culturally dependent) to the representational (culturally dependent) level. It would perhaps be replaced at the automatic-sequential level by a test of auditory closure such as that represented by a sound blending test, which would be independent of a particular language.

(2) A second question often asked is, "To what extent is this test unfair to the children from cultural backgrounds in which linguistic patterns differ somewhat from those used by the standardization population?" This subtest does indeed discriminate against certain subgroups, particularly Negro children who have been underexposed to certain linguistic patterns -- especially plurals and past tenses of verbs. This is a consideration which must enter into the clinical interpretation of the subtest when it is administered to a child from any environment in which grammatical usage is strikingly different from that found in the standardization population. It is hoped that someday separate norms will be available for use in such cases. In the meantime, it is important to recognize that the child who does not use middle-class grammar is, in reality, handicapped and the test should reveal this. The tester must be prepared to distinguish the child who receives a low score because he has learned the deviant grammar he has heard from the child whose low score reflects that he has ***not*** learned the grammar he has heard.

Visual Decoding

This test measures the ability to do conceptual matching, or to interpret meaningful pictures. An extreme deficit in this ability would perhaps resemble what has medically been called visual agnosia. At one time there was a feeling that this subtest might correlate with reading ability. Subsequent research and thinking has indicated that this is not the case. In fact, children with severe disabilities in reading tend to do well on this subtest. This indicates the importance of viewing the test as measuring the ability to interpret the pictures, objects, and other visual presentations ***excluding*** the printed word. A slight memory factor appears in this test, but only rarely appears to substantially affect a child's performance.

HINTS FOR ADMINISTRATION AND SCORING. The only problem consistently encountered with this subtest, and it is a minor one, is the occasional necessity to ask a youngster who is verbalizing the stimulus picture when he views it to refrain from such verbalization. If the first time such verbalization occurs, the examiner says "No, you don't have to name it, just look at it," this tendency to verbalize can usually be stopped. It is desirable to stop such verbalization because if the child persists in naming the stimulus picture he may then make the response on the basis of his auditory memory rather than on the basis of visual comprehension.

QUESTIONS OFTEN ASKED ABOUT THIS SUBTEST. The only question consistently asked regarding visual decoding is, "What was the basis for deciding which response picture was the correct one?" In the standardization of the test the correct response was designated as that response chosen by a certain majority of the children. Viewed in this light, one can argue that for a few items the test actually measures conformity rather than visual decoding. If one is testing a bright, creative child who seems to give deviant responses on some of the more difficult items, it is possible to go back at the completion of the test and question him regarding some of these responses. If such a procedure is followed the results should be noted clinically rather than normatively.

Motor Encoding

The motor encoding subtest was intended to measure the subject's ability to express an idea by gestures. It is not to be confused with motor mimicry or pure physical agility. The emphasis is on the expression of a meaningful idea in a way which is understood by the recipient of such communication. Early clinical experience has suggested the possibility that there are a substantial number of "Strauss Syndrome" children who show a combination of deficits in visual decoding and motor encoding.

HINTS FOR ADMINISTRATION AND SCORING. A common source of difficulty in administering this subtest is a failure to "wean" the child from making responses on the test book itself. Another common difficulty is the failure to make a smooth transition from the objects used early in the test to the test book utilizing pictures. Both of these problems can be readily solved if the following procedure is followed carefully. At the conclusion of the visual decoding subtest, the test book of pictures should be left in easy reach of the examiner with the pages turned so that the motor encoding subtest can be readily found. After the administration of the items utilizing actual objects the examiner should, with no delay whatsoever, turn to the first test picture -- a pencil sharpener. Quickly say to the child in the same manner used for the test objects, "Now show me what you do with this." The child ***must*** be allowed an opportunity to respond to the pencil sharpener item and thus receive credit for the item. If he makes his response with his hands touching the booklet, this is credited. However, it is essential that the item then be repeated (after he has received credit) in such a way as to insure that the response is not made on the book itself. If the examiner will remove the book and picture from the child's sight and repeat to him, "That was fine -- now pretend that you have the pencil sharpener right there in front of you and show me again how you would do it," this problem can be solved. With reticent children, especially girls in the six-to nine-year-old range, it is often desirable to introduce the test with some kind of remarks about the "Show me" game that is about to be played, indicating that it might seem a bit funny, but we'll play it . . ., etc.

Some particular items in this test are noteworthy: (#5) ***Drill***. If the child questions what this is, it is perhaps better not to tell him, although naming the object is generally permissible on motor encoding. If he misperceives the stimulus object as an eggbeater, he will be more likely to respond correctly than if he is told it is a drill; (# 7) ***Safe.*** The door of the safe should not be open, as many children misperceive this item as a refrigerator. For this reason and others, if the item is named by the examiner ("Now show me what you do with this ***safe***") more children tend to respond appropriately; (# 11) ***Funnel.*** Naming the funnel is also desirable, although many children (presumably more than in the standardization group) seem to be totally unfamiliar with this object.

In scoring motor encoding, it has been found that the examiner must watch especially carefully for the responses to item #6, the saw, and item #12, the stethoscope. On the saw item children frequently place the left arm on the table in such a way that it is impossible to determine whether they are holding the board as they saw with the right hand. If the child is asked to stand up or stretch before being presented with this item it is easier to determine whether his response includes holding the board. On the stethoscope item, one must carefully observe listening responses which involve listening in the air or listening to the table. It is not necessary that the child place the stethoscope over his own heart in order to receive credit.

QUESTIONS OFTEN ASKED ABOUT THIS SUBTEST. The most common question asked about motor encoding involves the extent to which the inclusion of many musical instruments affects the validity of this test for children who come from non-musical or highly musical backgrounds. These musical items were included in the test because in the standardization population it was found that they discriminated most successfully between the various age levels. In individual cases the examiner might want to make clinical notations indicating the extent to which the particular background might have affected the child's performance on some of these items.

Auditory-Vocal Association

This is an analogies test much like those found on the Binet and WISC. Clinical experience at this point suggests that this subtest is highly correlated with mental age. At the present time, this subtest and visual-motor association have a singular place of honor in the ITPA model, in that they alone occupy the entire area between the input and output of language. (For further discussion see pages 17 - 22).

HINTS FOR ADMINISTRATION AND SCORING. The only difficulties found in auditory-vocal association involve item #6. It has been found that this item is quite difficult and it is highly recommended that the subtest be begun with item #8 or # 1, but not with #6 as recommended in the manual. If a child persists in attempting to say the item along with the examiner, as many younger or retarded children do, it is necessary to say, "Wait until I am through, then you finish it." If the child is not discouraged from saying the item with the examiner, he very often will either fail to remember the structure given by the first part of the item or not have grasped the relationship.

Visual-Motor Sequential

This subtest of immediate visual memory for discrete, ordered stimuli appears to be one of the more important subtests in the diagnosis of some learning disabilities. There is a slight suggestion, based on an unpublished pilot study, that deficits in visual-motor sequencing may be related to poor reading, but that the converse is not true necessarily. That is, good reading may be associated with strong performance in auditory-vocal sequential, rather than with visual-motor sequential. (See Chapter 3).

HINTS FOR ADMINISTRATION AND SCORING. The five-second exposure time suggested in the manual poses a problem. When do the five seconds begin? The examiner should place the chips with maximum efficiency and rapidity, completing the verbal instructions as he does so. Then, the five-second exposure would begin on completion of the chip sequence. Distraction caused by the examiner's mixing the chips after dumping can be minimized if the tray is picked up from the end rather than the side, thereby mixing the chips as they are dumped. The manual should be studied thoroughly to insure proper placement of chips and tray in relation to examiner and subject.

QUESTIONS OFTEN ASKED ABOUT THIS SUBTEST. The inevitable question is "Must the test be so long and tedious?" The only answer is that examiner efficiency must be maximized to minimize the presentation time required.

A second question concerns the extent to which children might approach the task on a representational level by supplying verbal mediators. Data are not yet available on this, but at the present time one can cogently argue that the examiner is primarily interested in how well the child can handle the task, regardless of how he does it. If he does use verbal mediators on the subtest, he probably also does this in his everyday contact with similar "non-representational" material. Thus, the subtest is representative of his approach to real tasks involving visual memory.

Vocal Encoding

The vocal encoding subtest assesses the child's ability to verbally present meaningful ideas in response to a simple visual stimulus.

HINTS FOR ADMINISTRATION AND SCORING. Examiners often fail to question appropriately and to obtain maximum responses from the child. A helpful procedure is to ***fully*** utilize the demonstration item by insuring (through leading questions) that the child discuss the demonstration marble in terms of name, shape, color, uses, composition, etc. Then, before leaving the demonstration item, review all the child has said, emphasizing the category--e.g., "You told me its name, its color, its shape, etc."

Disregard the "one-minute" guide line suggested in the manual. This has been misleading with clinical cases, presumably because it was derived from experience with the "normal" standardization population. The experienced examiner will obtain more appropriate clues as to when the responses are exhausted from the child than from a watch.

QUESTIONS OFTEN ASKED ABOUT THE SUBTEST. There is some concern about the fact that only the quantity of responses, not the quality, is taken into account in scoring. This, of course, can and should be noted clinically.

Auditory-Vocal Sequential

No major problems have been found in this digit repetition test. Most examiners are quite comfortable with it after mastering the ½ second interval, probably because digit repetition tests are very familiar.

Visual-Motor Association

The ITPA test manual and other early publications state that visual-motor association is a measure of the ability to make relationships among the meaningful visual symbols which are presented. A legitimate question can be raised concerning whether this truly reflects the intention of this subtest. Perhaps it would be more desirable if the subtest had been intended to, or did in fact, measure the extent to which meaningful associations can be made among stimuli which in the subject's past experience have been visually associated.

HINTS FOR ADMINISTRATION AND SCORING. No major problems have been encountered with this subtest. It should perhaps be pointed out, however, that the "right" response was determined in the same way that it was for the visual decoding subtest, namely, that the correct response is that given by a certain majority of the standardization subjects. For this reason, as was pointed out with visual decoding, it can be argued that to some extent, this is a test of the conformity of association rather than logicality. For example, on item # 10, some children respond that the book, rather than the table, goes with the lamp. Such an association is both logical and visually acquired, but is nonetheless incorrect.

QUESTIONS OFTEN ASKED ABOUT THIS SUBTEST. The most common question asked is, "What does performance on this subtest mean diagnostically?" At the present time, this writer cannot give an answer. The subtest does not seem to correspond in all cases to the general pattern obtained on the visual channel, a finding which is statistically possible in that the subtests are not highly intercorrelated, but logically somewhat difficult. A substantial number of cases have been seen in which large deficits were noted in auditory-vocal automatic, auditory-vocal sequential and visual-motor association. This pattern of deficits has occurred often enough that considerable speculation has gone on concerning it. A possibility is that the visual-motor association subtest might in some cases be related to a visual closure or visual automatic function which is not presently assessed by the ITPA and which might be related to the automatic-sequential subtest mentioned above.

Auditory Decoding
This test assesses how well the child understands the spoken word.

HINTS FOR ADMINISTRATION AND SCORING. The only problems frequently encountered here involve a failure to encourage the child to respond yes or no, even when it is quite apparent that he has no comprehension of the vocabulary involved. It is necessary to encourage a response because this was the procedure followed with the standardization group. A minor consideration is the starting place for this test. Many children seem to find it easier to begin with the impersonal items -- "Do airplanes fly?" "Do cars cry?" -- than with the earlier personal items, such as "Do you rain?" For this reason it is acceptable practice to start with test item #5, preceded by the appropriate demonstration items. Many examiners allow credit beyond the ceiling item and obtain scores too high.

QUESTIONS OFTEN ASKED ABOUT THIS SUBTEST. Many persons feel that the vocabulary is not accurately graded. There is also dissatisfaction with the extent to which children are forced to guess at the upper ranges of the test. The answer to both of these questions or objections is that the test was standardized in its present form and the responses of subjects are being compared to the standardization group which encountered the same difficulties of vocabulary and guessing. Although the statistical rationale is sound, the test is logically troublesome to some.

PREREQUISITES TO PROFILE INTERPRETATION

The first prerequisite to interpreting the ITPA is that the subtests be properly administered and scored. In addition to the specific suggestions just outlined for each subtest, the following general considerations can be noted.

1. The demonstration items on all subtests should be thoroughly utilized, or even added to, to insure that in all cases the nature of the subtest task has been taught before testing begins. These demonstration items may be used in any way the examiner desires to insure maximum test performance. Vocal encoding, motor encoding, and auditory-vocal automatic are particularly affected.
2. On all subtests except vocal and motor encoding, the ceiling is to be obtained first, and then the basal if necessary. Examiners should be completely familiar with the requirements for ceiling and basal levels on all subtests so that over-testing and under-testing will be eliminated. Auditory decoding, visual decoding, and visual-motor association pose special problems.
3. The examiner must be completely familiar with scoring on all subtests so that ceilings and basals can be recognized immediately and so that items are not invalidated by improper questioning or failure to question.
4. Knowledge of what constitutes the psycholinguistic ability being measured by a given subtest should be the guideline in making decisions pertaining to problems in test administration. If, for example, the examiner is thoroughly aware that motor encoding is assessing the subject's ability to demonstrate how an object is used, ***given*** that he can decode the object (knows what the object is), the examiner would then know that he can name the object for the child if necessary. Similarly he would know which items could be repeated if necessary, etc.

This list by no means exhausts the possible test administration problems but it does cover the most serious and most frequent. Profiles obtained by examiners who need more practice in administration and scoring, frequently are characterized by a peak in auditory decoding (missed the ceiling) and a dip in vocal decoding (inadequate use of demonstration item). Once it has been established that the obtained scores represent those actually earned by the subject under standardized testing procedures, the first prerequisite to interpreting the ITPA has been met.

The second prerequisite for interpretation is actually an extension of the first -- i.e., the profile must be checked for internal consistency. This is a broad and difficult assignment and one about which even the most experienced ITPA clinician continually learns more. In essence it amounts to asking, "Does this profile make sense? Could a child look like this?" One straw-man problem which need not cause particular concern in this respect is the "logical" relationship among decoding, association, and encoding. Psychologists frequently ask how a child can possibly score higher in association or encoding than in decoding. There is an assumption that decoding must somehow set a ceiling on what or how much can be associated or encoded. This may or may not be true; but it does not apply to the ITPA for the simple reason that the decoding tests are not exhaustive. That is, a subject may be very adequately receiving information in ways not assessed by the ITPA and then, in turn, be associating and encoding in ways that are measured. One need only keep in mind Helen Keller's possible profile. She would obviously be unable to score at all on either decoding test and yet would exceed norms on encoding.

A related issue is that of the independence of the subtests from each other, or to put it another way, of the language factors in the test and their structural relationship to each other. Most, if not all, of the factor analytic studies which have been done have used either normal or mentally retarded subjects. It seems possible that if such studies were ultimately to reveal only three or four, or even only one general language factor, the diagnostic use of the ITPA with children who by definition have deviant language patterns would not be affected. Perhaps for most children, a particular subtest is heavily dependent upon or related to another, but this does not lessen the usefulness of the ITPA with the very child for whom this is not the case.

While internal consistency of a profile does not mean that decoding must always be the highest score or that certain test scores must always fall into a given relationship with other tests, it is more difficult to spell out what it does mean. Perhaps a cautious approach is to suggest that certain patterns are seen time and time again, while others are so rare as to cause question. Examples of very rare profiles would include: severe deficiency in visual decoding coupled with high motor encoding; very high peaks in both association subtests; auditory-vocal automatic very high if the child is other than gifted; a deficiency on all auditory-vocal subtests except vocal encoding or on all visual-motor subtests except motor encoding; a pattern of several unrelated deficiencies such as auditory decoding, visual-motor association, auditory-vocal automatic and visual-motor sequential.

The last prerequisite to interpreting an ITPA profile is the determination that it is basically consistent with the child's daily behavior as reported by teachers and parents. If it is not, in all probability it is the test's sample of behavior that is unreliable, not the "every-day" sample. If a teacher reports, e.g., that the child is very hesitant to respond in class and does so in single words if at all, the examiner should anticipate a vocal encoding deficit. When the clinician becomes thoroughly familiar with the test and the behaviors it samples, he should be able to plot a reasonably accurate profile just from descriptions of the child's behavior without actually administering the test. Far from making the test itself unnecessary, the fact that experienced clinicians can do this points up how well the test does correspond to relevant educational behaviors and it highlights the usefulness of the test as an initial diagnostic survey.

CHAPTER 2

ITPA PROFILES OF CERTAIN GROUPS OF CHILDREN

Before presenting profiles and interpretive considerations for individual children it seems pertinent to briefly review what has been found regarding certain types or groups of children.

The ITPA has been used in reasonably extensive research involving various groups of exceptional children and from these studies plus clinical experience it is possible to offer tentative generalizations about the typical profile for these types of exceptionality. In one sense these group profiles pose an old and persistent problem -- what frame of reference is most meaningful in evaluating test performances of children who differ from the standardization group? Since there is, for example, a typical profile for mongoloids, should the examiner respond to such a profile by saying, "What an unusual (compared to the norms) profile, with its peak in motor encoding, etc." or "What a typical (compared to other mongoloids) profile, it's just as expected?"

In a very limited sense, the group profiles* which follow can serve as norms for the groups depicted. Perhaps their greatest value beyond that of a frame of reference for the interpreter of individual profiles is that they might suggest certain bases for curriculum planning for the various groups.

Further research may well modify some of the profiles and they are offered here as tentative guides only.

*Many of the profiles presented in this section are from research studies reviewed in Bateman, Barbara, THE ITPA IN CURRENT RESEARCH, Urbana: Univer. of Illinois Press, 1965.

MENTALLY RETARDED CHILDREN

Figures 1, 2, 3, and 4 are composite profiles of groups of retarded and slow learning children and they depict what appear to be "typical" profiles for groups of retarded children whose mean IQs are near or below 75. The outstanding feature is a deficit in the entire automatic-sequential level, with visual-motor sequential frequently slightly higher than auditory-vocal sequential. At the representational level, a slight deficit is often seen in auditory-vocal association (e.g., Fig. 2). A slight preference for the visual-motor channel over the auditory-vocal channel is also very frequently seen, (e.g., Fig. 4) especially where environmental deprivation is involved in the retardation.

There are important educational implications to be derived from the knowledge of the basic deficit in automatic, habitual, or rote aspects of language usage in the retarded. The great need for repetition, over-learning, and "mechanical" drill is apparent. A danger inherent in current designs to make all learning situations "meaningful" to the child is that by so doing, the retarded child will handle these tasks at the representational level exclusively, thereby further strengthening his already strong representational skills and neglecting the automatic-sequential areas which are in need of exercise. The total effect of gearing the curriculum and teaching methods to the meaningful level is to thus increase the cognitive, linguistic discrepancies within the child.

Clinical experience has also indicated that many, if not most, retarded children do have some association difficulties (e.g., Fig. 1); The association process assessed by the ITPA might be described as a "retrieval" process, but from a theoretical vantage point association would also include an earlier categorization or generalization (concept formation) stage. Information is decoded, organized, and stored before it is "retrieved." Thus it is impossible to determine, on the basis of an ITPA auditory-vocal association deficit, whether the problem is in retrieval of material or in the earlier organization of material to be stored. The visual-motor association subtest is more heavily weighted with organization ("Which one goes with this?) however, and most of the profiles do not show as large a deficit in visual-motor (organization) as in auditory-vocal (retrieval) association. This suggests that many retarded children have a general retrieval problem, manifest in both the representational and automatic-sequential levels.

FIGURE 1

Mentally Retarded Boys - A

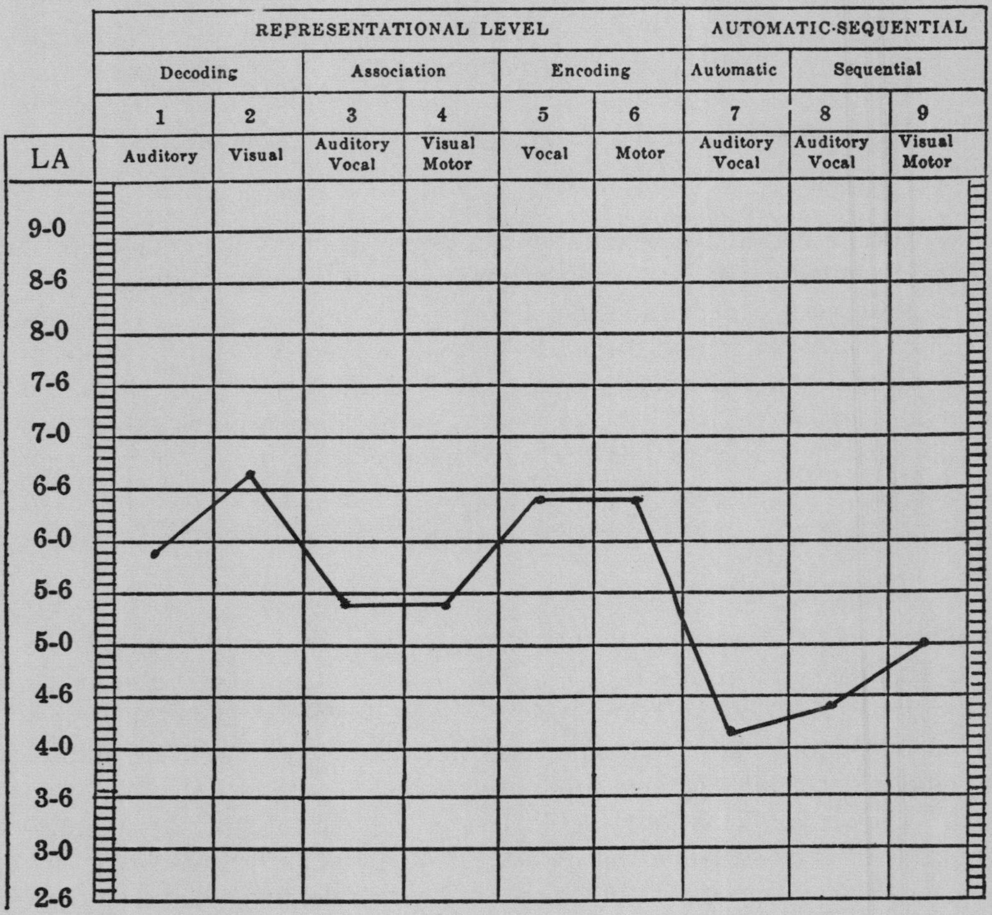

REPRESENTATIONAL LEVEL | AUTOMATIC-SEQUENTIAL

Decoding | Association | Encoding | Automatic | Sequential

1 Auditory | 2 Visual | 3 Auditory Vocal | 4 Visual Motor | 5 Vocal | 6 Motor | 7 Auditory Vocal | 8 Auditory Vocal | 9 Visual Motor

LA

9-0
8-6
8-0
7-6
7-0
6-6
6-0
5-6
5-0
4-6
4-0
3-6
3-0
2-6

N: 20
CAs: 6-0 to 12-0 years
IQs: 44 to 72
Reference: Wiseman, 1966.

FIGURE 2

Mentally Retarded Boys - B

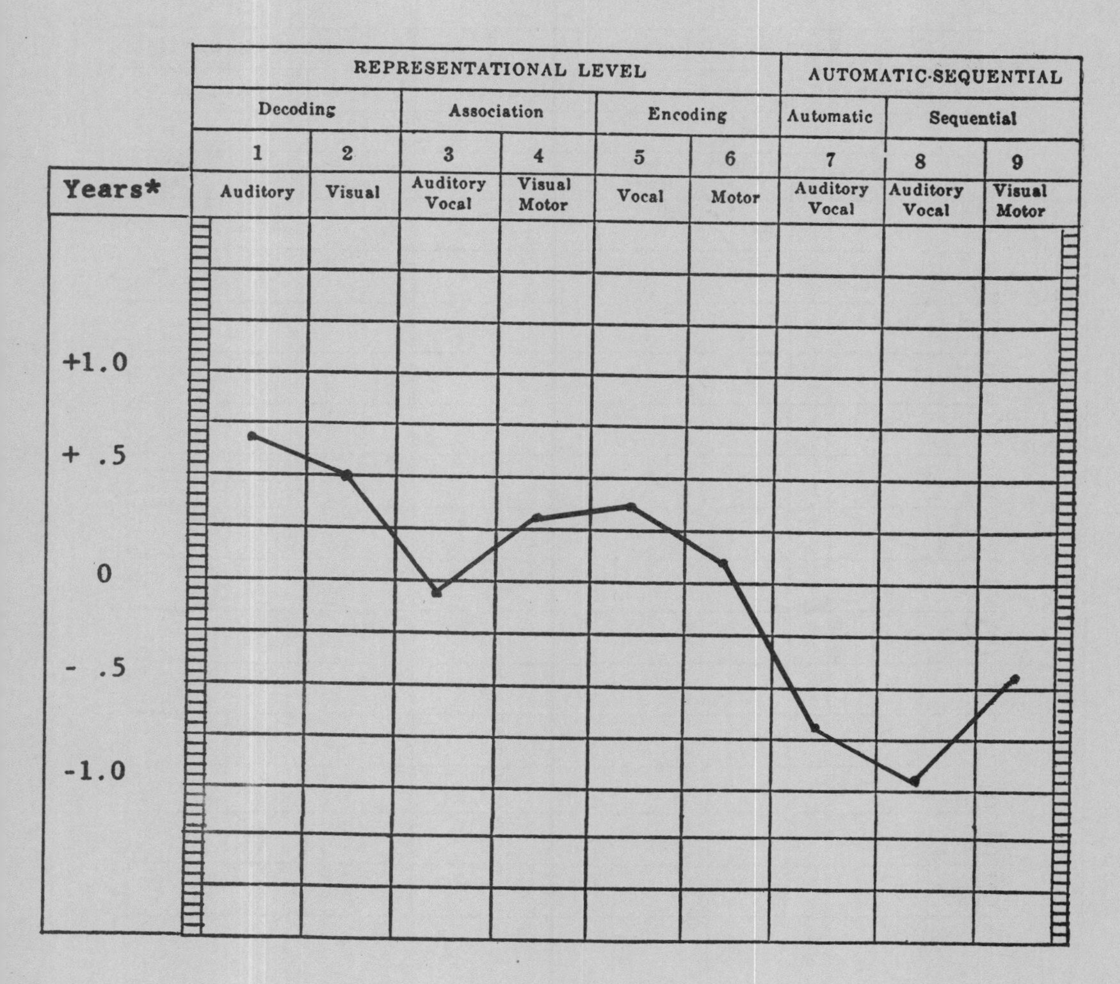

N: 25
CAs: 6-6 to 9-6 years
Mean IQ: Approximately 60
Reference: Bateman, 1967a

*Each subject's average language age was computed and his subtest score expressed as a deviation from his own mean language age. These deviation scores were averaged for the group.

FIGURE 3

Slow Learning Children

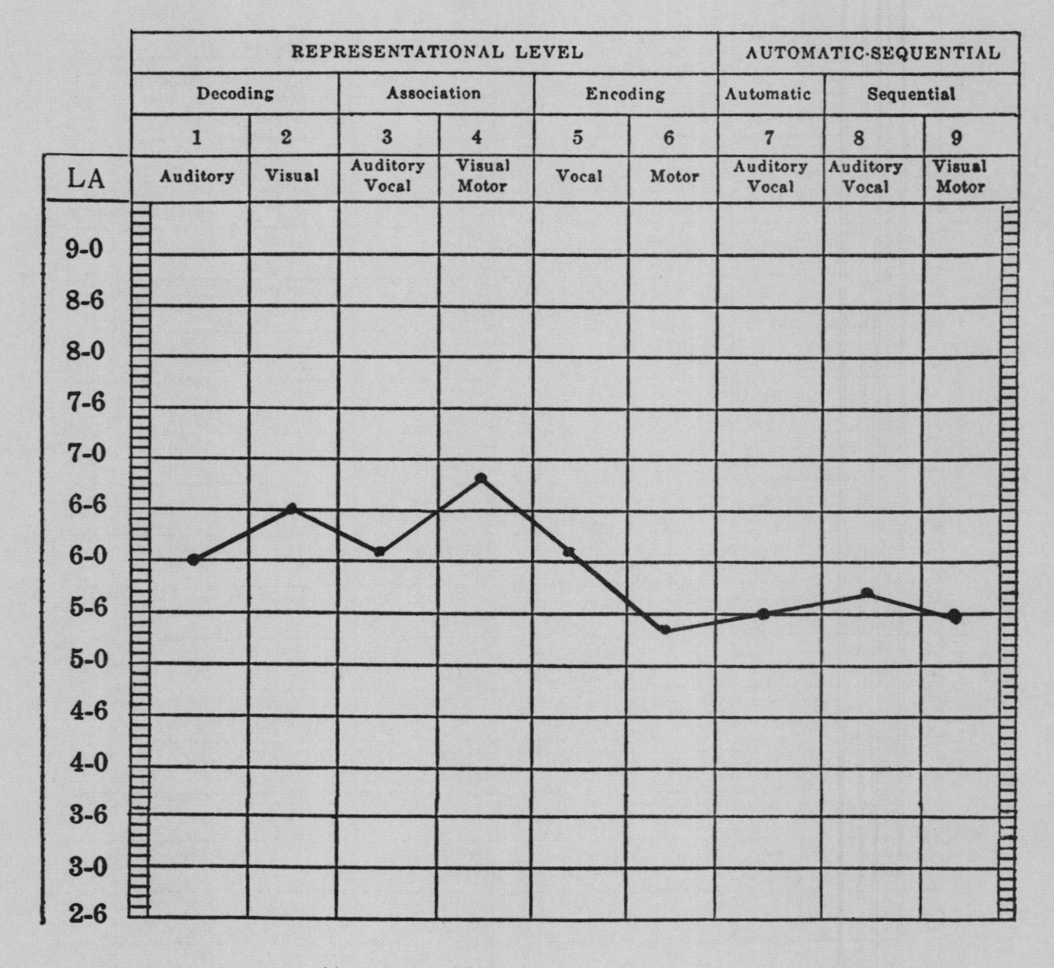

N: 89

Mean CA: 7-11 years

Mean MA: 6-7 years

Other: These children had been identified as EMH two years prior to ITPA testing, but at the time of ITPA testing their mean IQ was near 85.

Reference: Bateman & Wetherell, 1965.

FIGURE 4

Mongoloid and Non-mongoloid Retardates

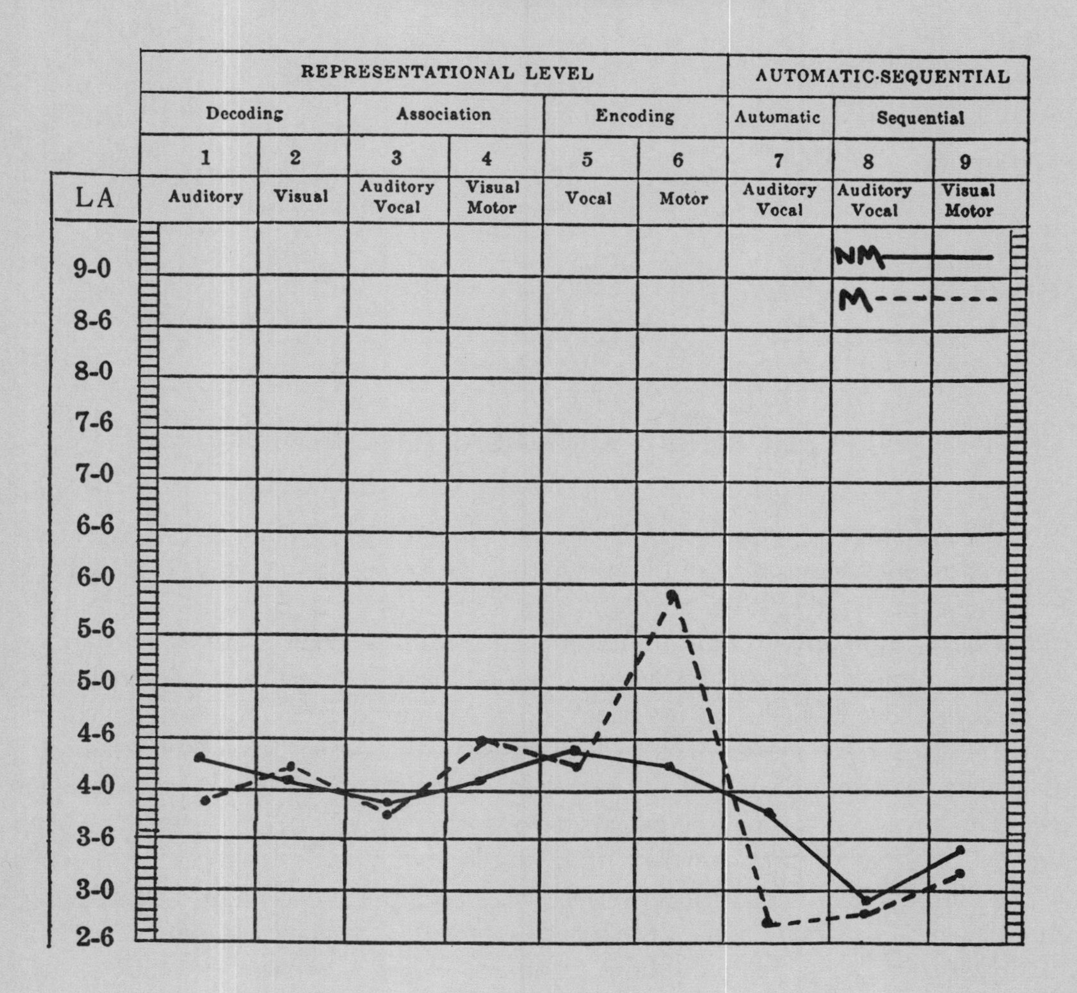

Mongoloids		Non-Mongoloids	
N:	30	N:	30
Mean MA:	4-1	Mean MA:	4-0
Mean CA:	9-4	Mean CA:	9-4
Mean IQ:	45.5	Mean IQ:	43.6

Other: Differences are significant on motor encoding and auditory-vocal automatic

Reference: McCarthy (in press)

PUBLIC SCHOOL KINDERGARTEN CHILDREN

Figure 5 presents two groups of public school kindergarten children, one group from an upper-middle and one from a lower-middle socio-economic status (SES) district. First, it can be noted that the profiles mirror each other on all subtests except visual-motor association and on motor encoding. The motor encoding performance of the lower SES subjects may well be due to a cultural bias in the test items. The relatively low performance of higher SES subjects on visual-motor association is to be expected since the correct answer on these test items is that answer given by the majority of the standardization subjects (as discussed in Chapter One). The more intelligent and/or creative subject may be penalized for a logical but atypical association. The higher SES subjects' strongest performance is in auditory-vocal association which is highly correlated with Binet mental age. The low SES subjects show a slight dip in auditory-vocal automatic which is also predictable due to the large number of "culturally disadvantaged children," both white and Negro, included in this population.

The mean mental age (Detroit test) of the higher SES subjects was 19½ months higher than that of the lower SES subjects. The higher SES subjects' superiority on the ITPA ranged from only eight months on visual-motor sequential to approximately two years on auditory decoding, auditory-vocal association, vocal encoding, auditory-vocal automatic, and motor encoding. The mean subtest difference between the two groups is 19½ months, exactly the same as the mean mental age difference. The greatest effect of SES status in these groups appears to be a positive relationship to auditory-vocal channel performance. In view of the heavy loading of verbal items in intelligence tests, and the high correlation between IQ and SES this finding was not unexpected.

The lower-middle SES subjects depicted in Figure 5 were grouped by sex, and the resulting profiles shown in Figure 6. The males are more variable among subtests and are slightly superior in decoding and encoding; the females slightly superior in association and sequencing. Perhaps association and sequencing are more closely related to school achievement, particularly reading in the early years, than are decoding and encoding.

In Figure 7 the same low-average SES subjects are grouped by race. The white and Negro subjects' profiles parallel each other in all areas except auditory-vocal automatic and sequential. The difference in overall elevation is directly related to a mental age difference. The substantial superiority of Negroes in auditory-vocal sequencing has been confirmed in many other studies.

The same male-female differences shown in Figure 5 were found in exaggerated degree among the Negro subjects, but are not presented here.

The profiles of normal kindergarten children are flat except for those exceptions or points discussed above. The flatness, combined with the predictable and reasonable exceptions, strongly supports the accuracy of the test norms.

FIGURE 5

Kindergarten Children -- Socio-economic Status

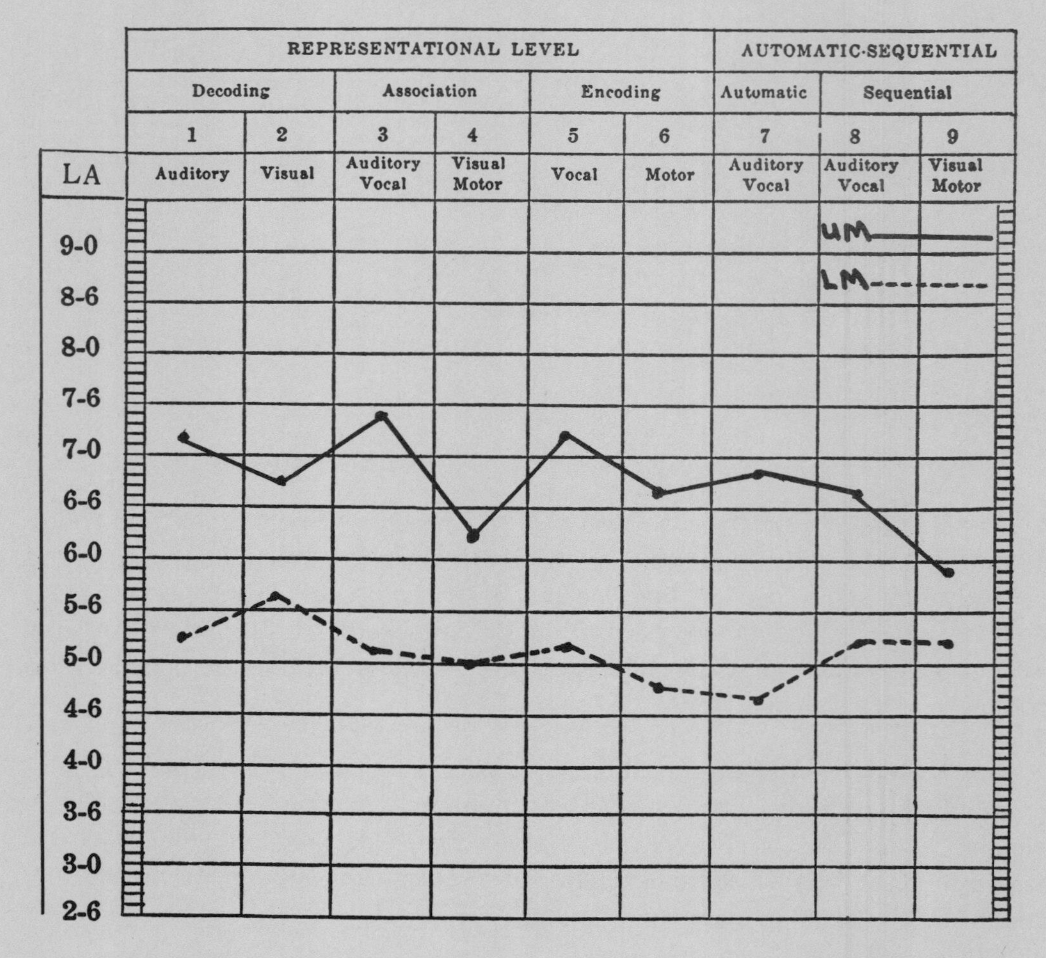

Upper-middle Class		Lower-middle Class	
N:	50	N:	105
Mean CA:	5-9	Mean CA:	5-6
Mean IQ:	125	Mean IQ:	98

Reference: Bateman, 1964.

FIGURE 6

Kindergarten Children - Sex

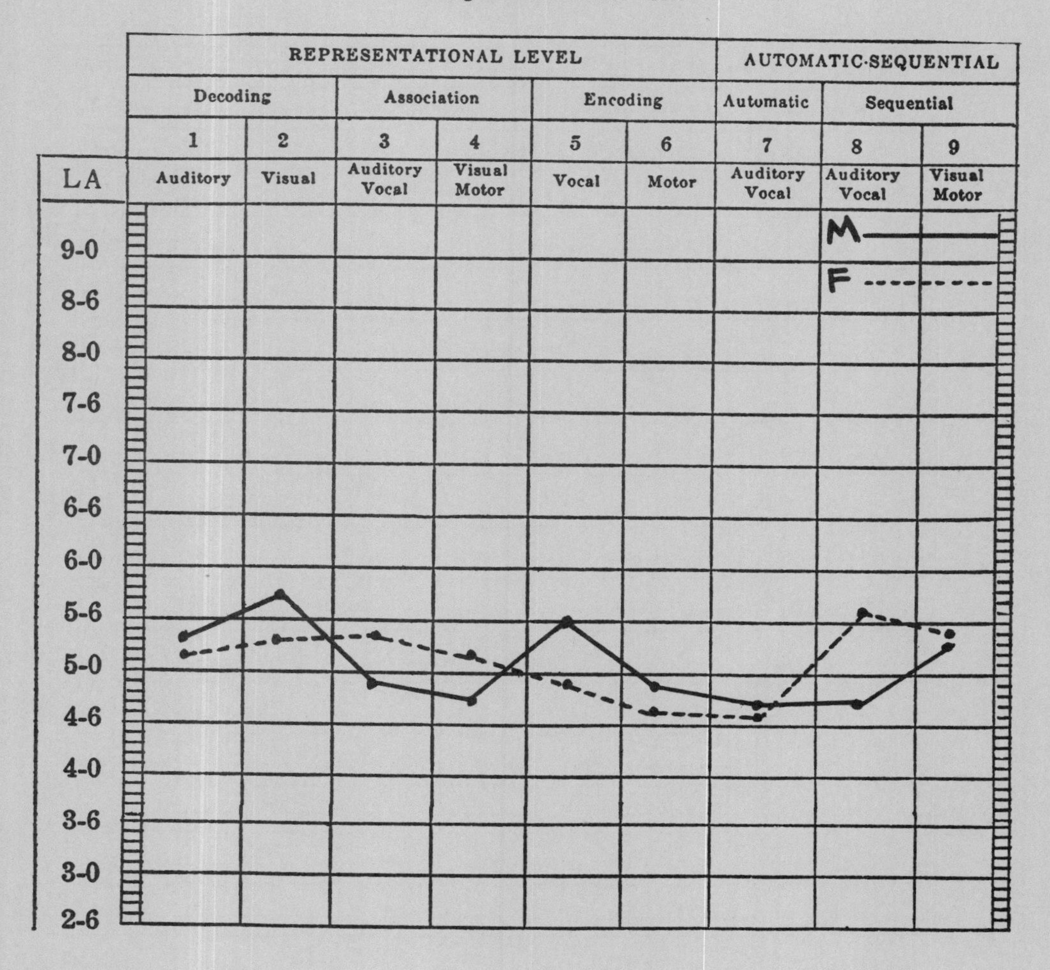

Males		Females	
N:	51	N:	63
Mean IQ:	96.4	Mean IQ:	98.6

Reference: Bateman, 1964.

FIGURE 7

Kindergarten Children - Race

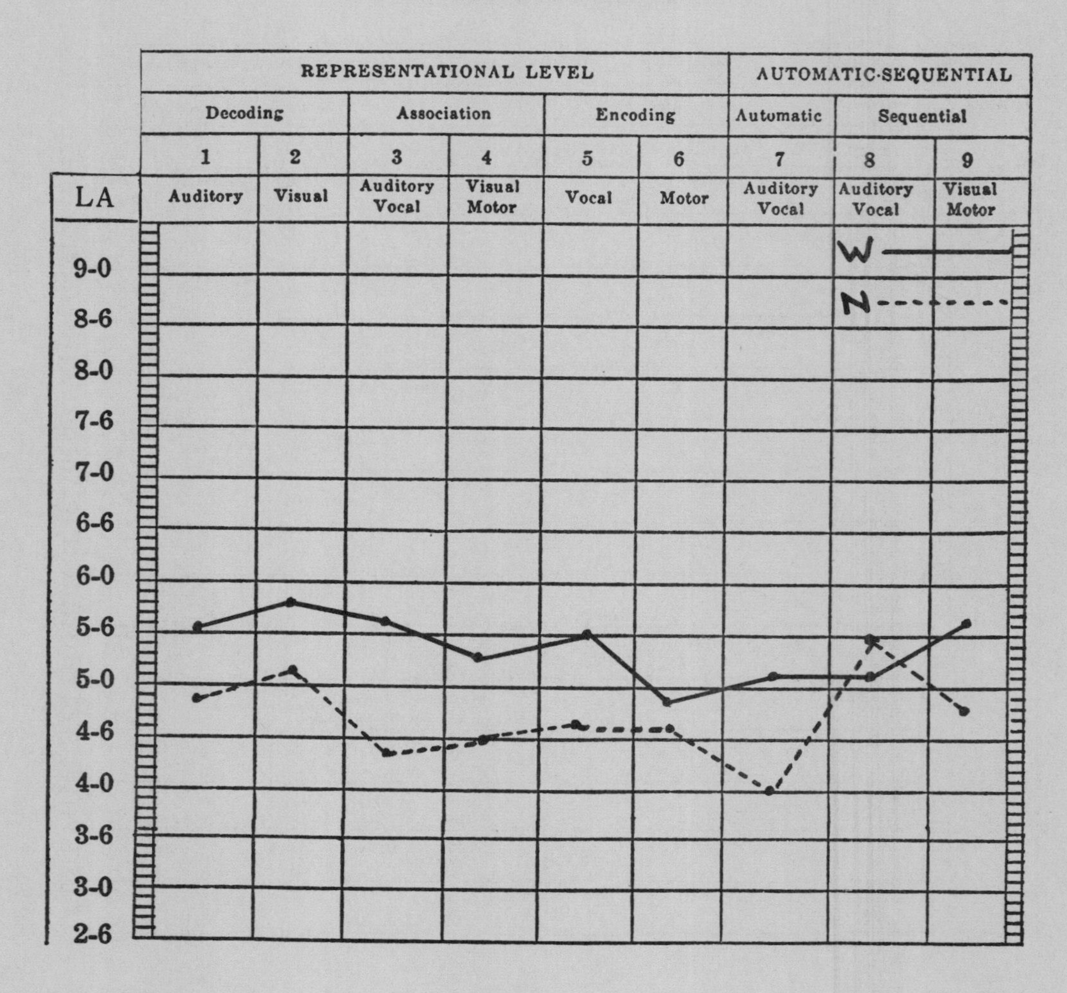

White		Negro	
N:	70	N:	44
Mean IQ:	103	Mean IQ:	89

Reference: Bateman, 1964.

CULTURALLY DISADVANTAGED

The outstanding feature of the ITPA profile of young, culturally disadvantaged Negro children, is the peak in auditory-vocal sequential (see Fig. 8 and 9). Visual-motor association is also high in both profiles. Auditory-vocal automatic is an area of relative weakness since scoring is based on the grammatical patterns of the white standardization sample. A preference for the visual-motor channel is clear. Few other profiles for groups of disadvantaged children have yet appeared in the literature, but wide clinical evidence supports this basic profile for the disadvantaged group.

Language development is in general somewhat below age level for these youngsters. This suggests that early education for the culturally disadvantaged should be heavily weighted with language experiences, as is the current practice. Ways of utilizing auditory memory should be explored.

FIGURE 8

Culturally Disadvantaged Negro Children - A

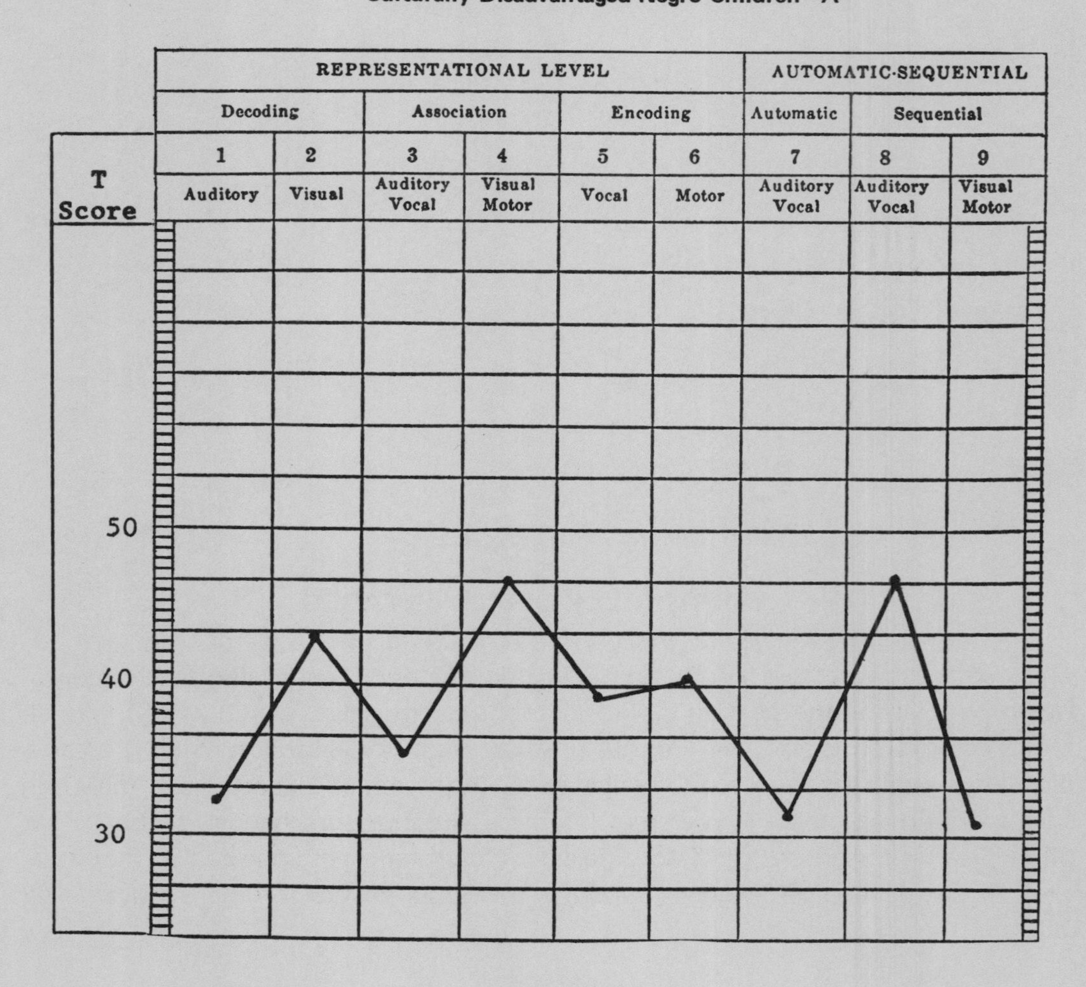

N: 18
Mean IQ: 83.4
Mean MA: 54.5 months
Reference: Weaver, 1963.

FIGURE 9

Culturally Disadvantaged Negro Children - B

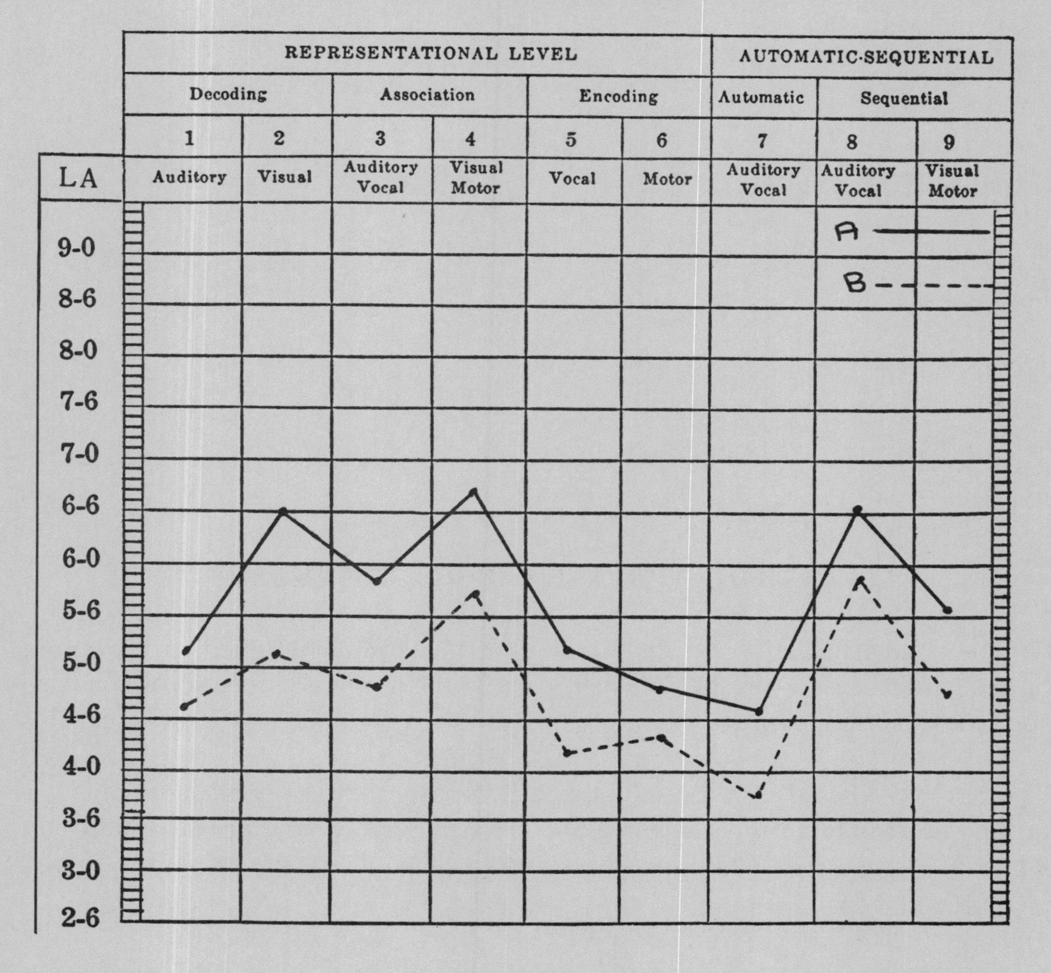

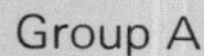

Group A

N: 42
CA Range: 5-6 to 6-6 years
Mean IQ: Approximately 95

Group B

N: 47
CA Range: 5-6 to 6-6 years
Mean IQ: Approximately 83

Reference: Klaus, 1965.

ARTICULATION AND LANGUAGE PROBLEMS

Children with articulation defects (Fig. 10 and 11) have slight deficits in the automatic sequential level. A slight deficiency across the entire auditory-vocal channel is also suggested by Figure 10.

Figure 11 was based only on males, and it appears that the obtained profile is reflecting this sex factor or that the group mean IQ was somewhat below 100. Or, it is just possible that articulation problems do psycholinguistically resemble mild mental retardation (see Figure 3).

A study comparing slow learners who have articulation problems with slow learners who do not have any speech problems could clarify this area.

While the ITPA does statistically differentiate deaf and sensory aphasic on certain subtests, (see Figs. 12 and 13) it does not provide an easy differential diagnosis for an individual child. Both groups show the predictably severe auditory-vocal channel problem. High motor encoding is frequently a good clue to check auditory acuity.

FIGURE 10

Children with Moderate to Severe Articulation Defects

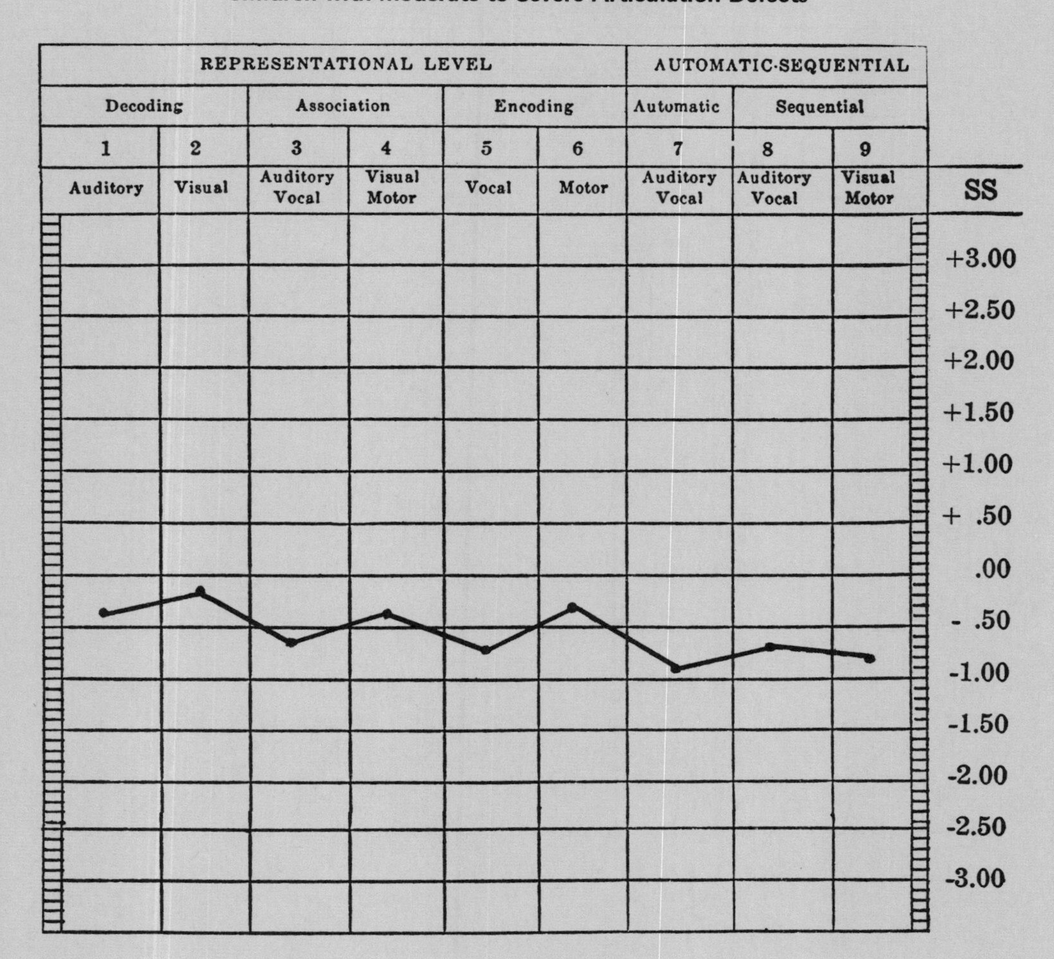

N: 40
CA Range: 6-0 to 7-0 years
Mean IQ: 98 (PPVT)

Reference: Ferrier, 1966.

FIGURE 11

Males with Persistent Articulation Defects

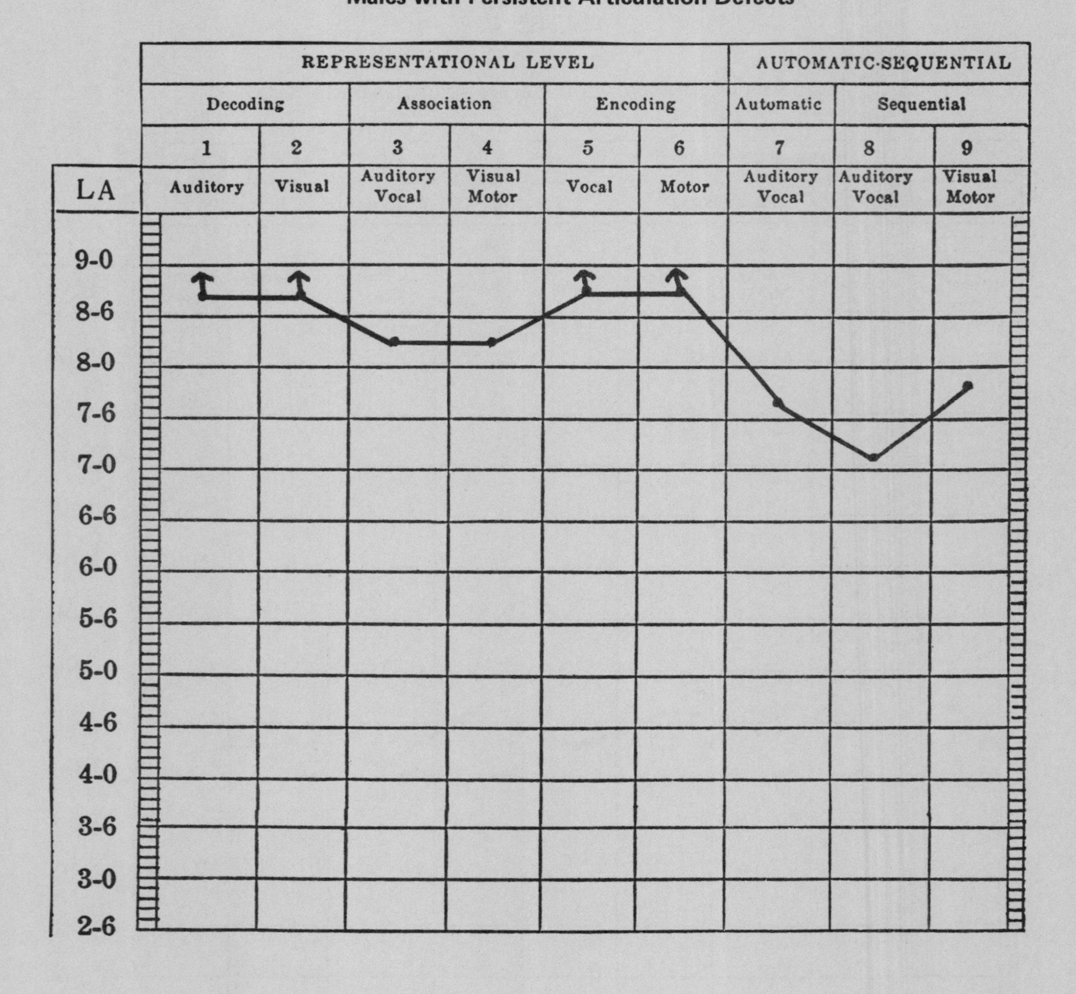

N:	18 males
CA Range:	7-0 to 9-0 years
IQ Range:	90 to 110
Other:	These subjects had all had 16 months of speech therapy and had not made improvement.

Reference: Foster, 1963.

OTHER EXCEPTIONAL CHILDREN

The following comments are offered tentatively and are based as much upon clinical experience as on the research from which most of the profiles are drawn. In some cases the selection of group profiles was made from among several studies. In each case the profile believed most representative of clinical findings was chosen.

Visually Handicapped

Visual impairment milder than 20/70 does not appear to substantially affect ITPA performance (see Fig. 14) except possibly in visual memory. This is probably as much related to slow perception as to memory ***per se.*** A definite visual channel disability, most severe in visual decoding, is seen in legally blind subjects. But even so, the visual-channel problem is not as severe as most would probably anticipate.

Cerebral Palsy

The striking contrast between the profiles of spastics and athetoids (Fig. 15) cannot but cause speculation concerning differential neurological damage. The spastics' profile is the only one known to this reviewer in which a relative deficiency is seen at the representational level.

Gifted

Intellectually gifted children (Fig. 16) usually score higher on the auditory-vocal channel, especially on auditory-vocal association and auditory-vocal automatic, than on the visual-motor channel. Visual memory seems more closely related to CA than to MA.

Reading Disabilities

Many children with severe reading problems show a peak in visual decoding and/or motor encoding and a deficiency in auditory memory. A deficiency in visual memory is almost as likely to occur. Less frequently, deficiencies in auditory-vocal automatic are also seen. (See following chapter for profiles and further discussion).

FIGURE 12

Deafness and Sensory Aphasia

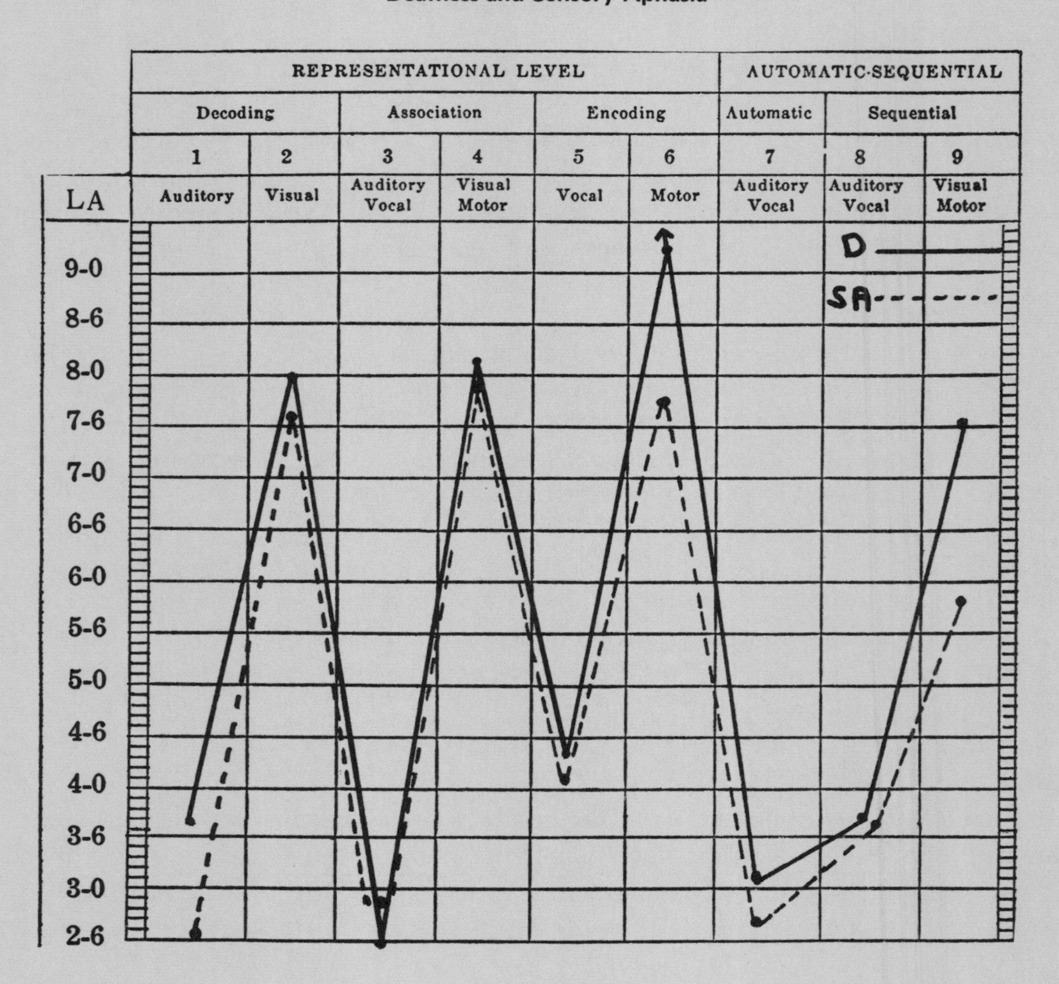

N: 25 Deaf, 17 Sensory-Aphasic
CAs: 5-0 to 9-6 years
IQs: 80 to 120

Reference: Olson, 1961.

FIGURE 13

Hard-of-hearing and Receptive Aphasic Children

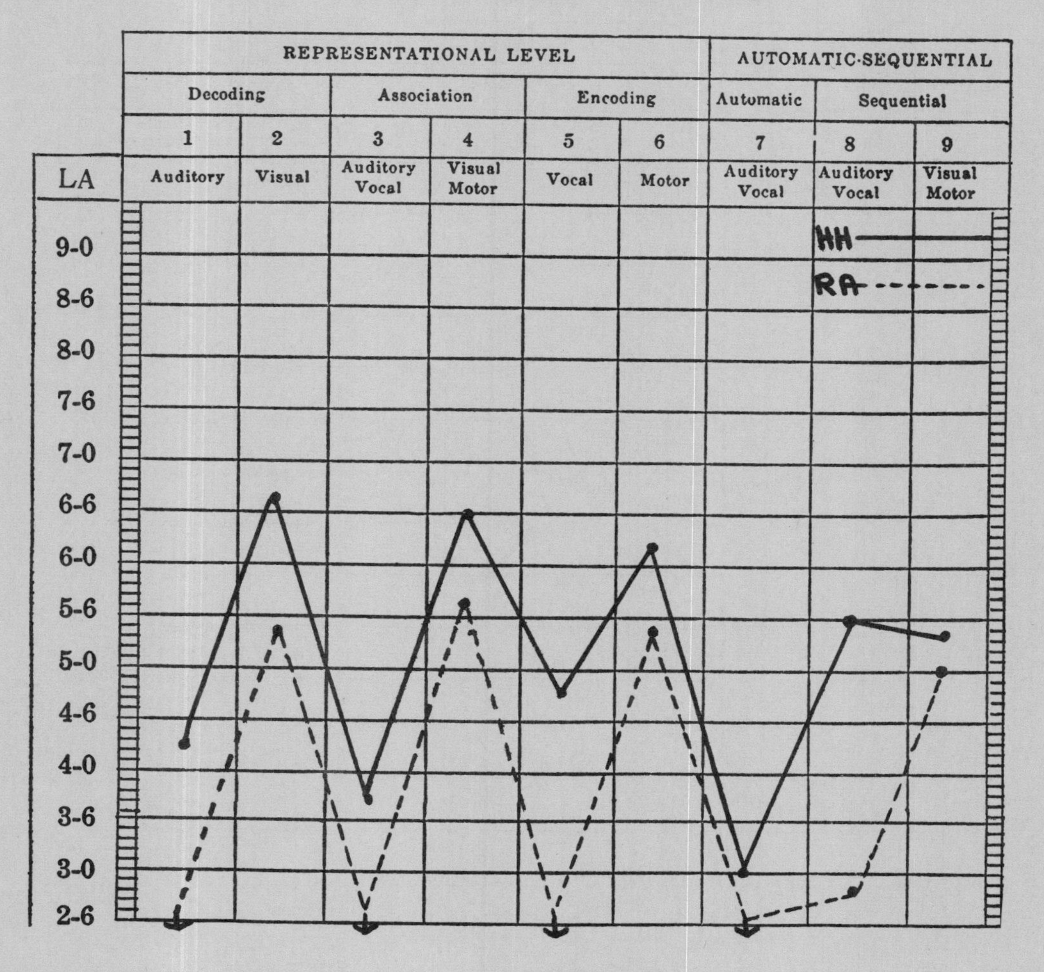

Hard-of-hearing		Receptive Aphasic	
N:	24	N:	24
Mean IQ:	107	Mean IQ:	102
CAs:	4-6 to 6-6 years	CAs:	4-6 to 6-6 years

Reference: Reichstein, 1963.

FIGURE 14

Legally Blind and Partially Seeing Children

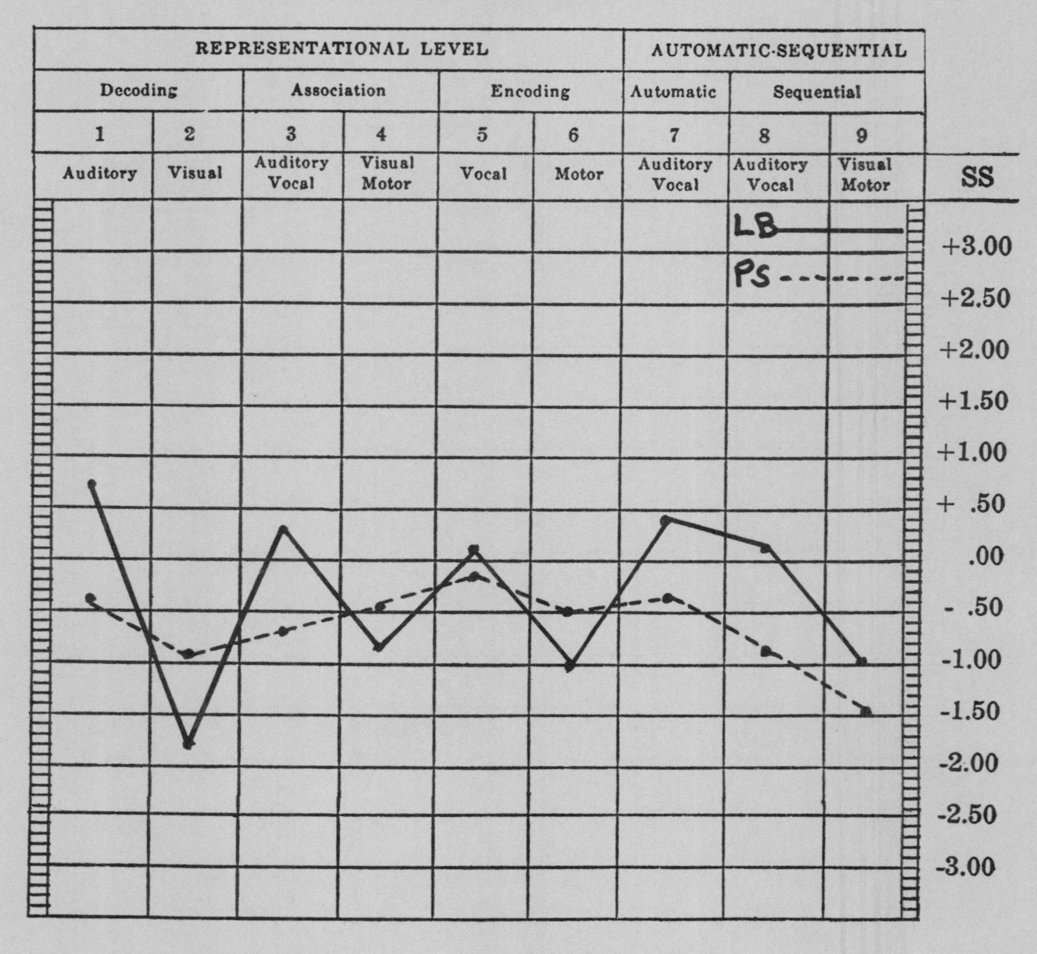

Legally Blind		Partially Seeing	
N:	24	N:	33
Mean IQ:	106	Mean IQ:	95

Other: All children were enrolled in grades 1 to 3 in public school programs for visually handicapped.

Reference: Bateman, 1963.

FIGURE 15

Cerebral Palsied Children

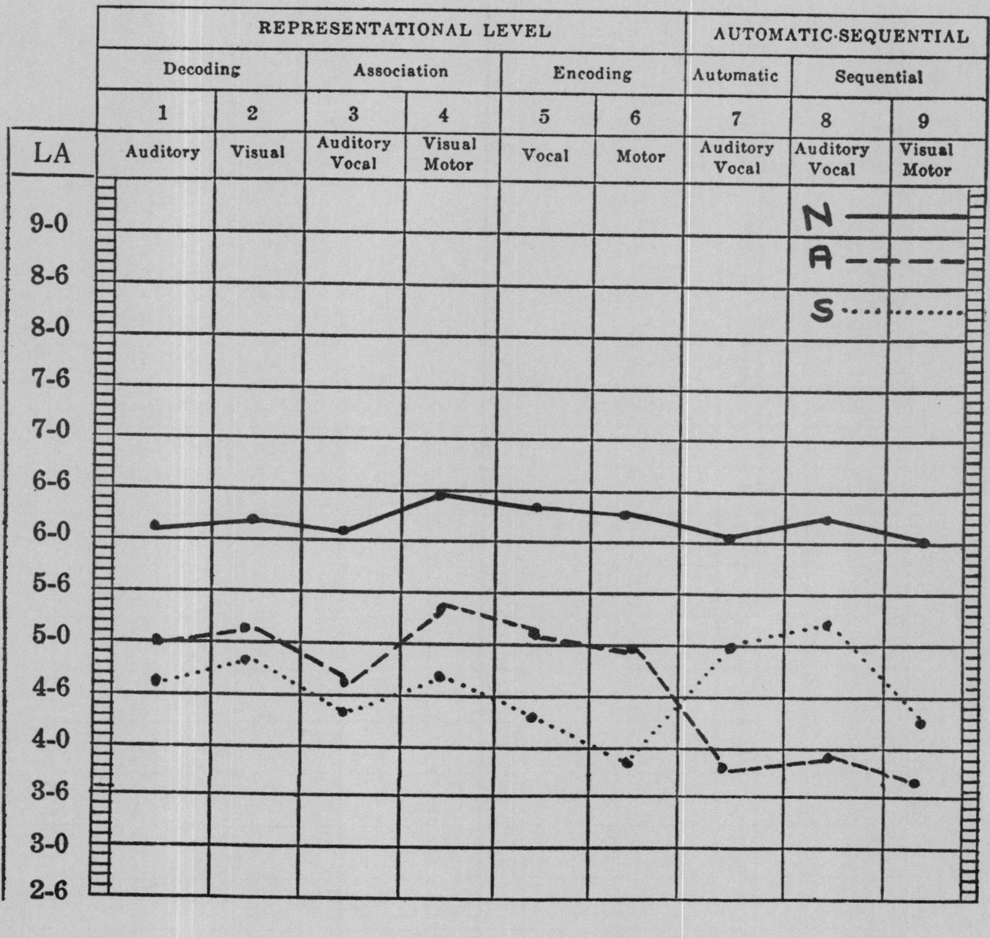

Normal

N: 32

Athetoid

N: 24

Spastic

N: 68

All Groups

CA: 4-0 to 9-0

MA: 3-4 to 9-0

IQ: above 80

Other: Children with severe visual or auditory defects were excluded. Note the reversal of patterns shown by athetoids and spastics and the flat control profile.

Reference: Myers, 1965.

FIGURE 16

Gifted Children

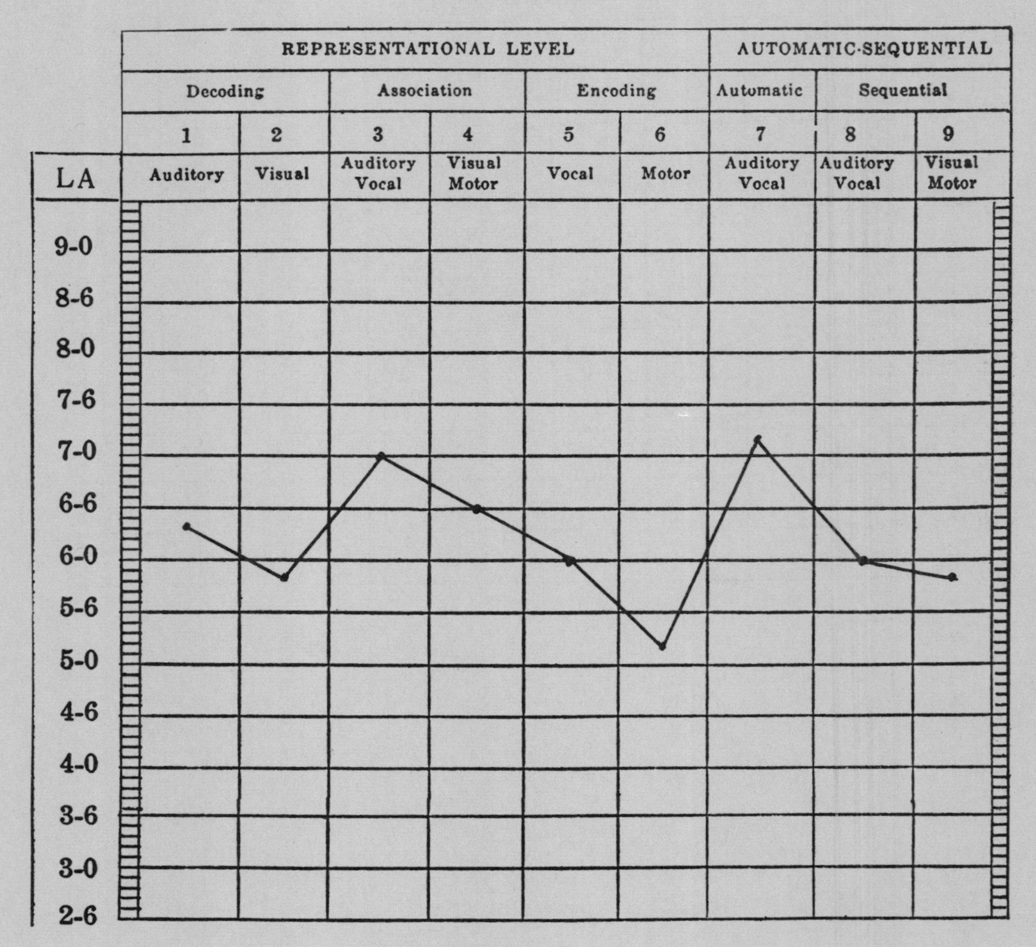

N: 21
Mean CA: 5-1 years
Mean IQ: 132.1

Reference: Mueller, 1964.

CHAPTER 3

THE ITPA AND READING

The ITPA performance of children with reading problems has been investigated in several studies (e.g., Kass, 1966; Bateman, 1963, 1967; Ragland, 1966) and the results are all highly consistent. Children with reading problems show deficiencies at the automatic-sequential level of psycholinguistic functioning. They frequently, but not necessarily, do well on the visual decoding and motor encoding subtests. These relationships and their implications for reading instruction have been explored elsewhere (Bateman, 1967).

The profiles of good and poor readers presented in this section* were obtained before the children entered school. Reading achievement was assessed one year later at the end of first grade. The same patterns of weaknesses and strengths which research has uncovered in older disabled readers show up in these younger children. While no hard data are presented here, the inference from these profiles is that some potential reading disabilities can be detected by the aware ITPA clinician and possibly prevented by early intervention.

The school system in which the children shown in Figures 17-21 were enrolled is primarily upper-middle class and the reading instruction is outstanding. The average reading level of the first-graders at the end of the year was almost third grade. The good and poor readers whose profiles are presented were selected from the highest and lowest ten percent of the first-graders studied (N = 240).

The design of the study required that some children be taught reading by an auditory method (Lippincott basal reading series) and some by a visual method (Scott, Foresman basal reading series).

*The study in which these profiles were obtained has been reported elsewhere (Bateman, 1967) and the author expresses deepest thanks to the Highland Park, Illinois School system for making the study possible.

POOR READERS

Of the 18 children with the lowest reading achievement at the end of first grade, 16 had been taught by the visual method and 2 by the auditory method. Figure 17 shows a poor reader who had excellent auditory memory and some weaknesses in motor encoding and visual memory. He was taught by the visual method and presumably was unable to use his auditory memory independently to learn word attack skills. His visual memory was not adequate to allow him to learn by the sight method.

Figure 18 shows a second poor reader taught by the visual method. His auditory memory is extremely weak. Grossly poor auditory memory seems to suggest poor reading, almost regardless of method. On the other hand, as shown in the preceding profile, even excellent auditory memory cannot always overcome the method. The peak in motor encoding seen in Figure 18 is frequently found in poor readers. Fourteen of the 18 poor readers had severe weaknesses in one of the memory tests. Only 3 of these poor readers had notably good auditory memory, but all these were taught by a visual method and were presumably unable to utilize the auditory memory to advantage. However, it seems reasonable to suppose that by the end of second grade these three will pick up phonic skills, regardless of teaching method. Conversely, the prognosis for those subjects weak in both memory areas seems poor regardless of method. These are the children for whom early introduction of a tactile approach to learning to read would seem reasonable.

GOOD READERS

Of the 16 highest achievers in reading, 14 had been taught by the auditory method. Figures 19-21 are typical of the good readers. All show excellent auditory memory and almost as strong visual memory. None has a peak in motor encoding.

The five profiles of good and poor readers all came from the same study and same school district, but are nevertheless broadly representative. The obvious correlation between the automatic-sequential level functions and reading has been shown in several research studies as mentioned above, but seems even more striking in clinical practice.

FIGURE 17

Poor Reader A - Visual Method

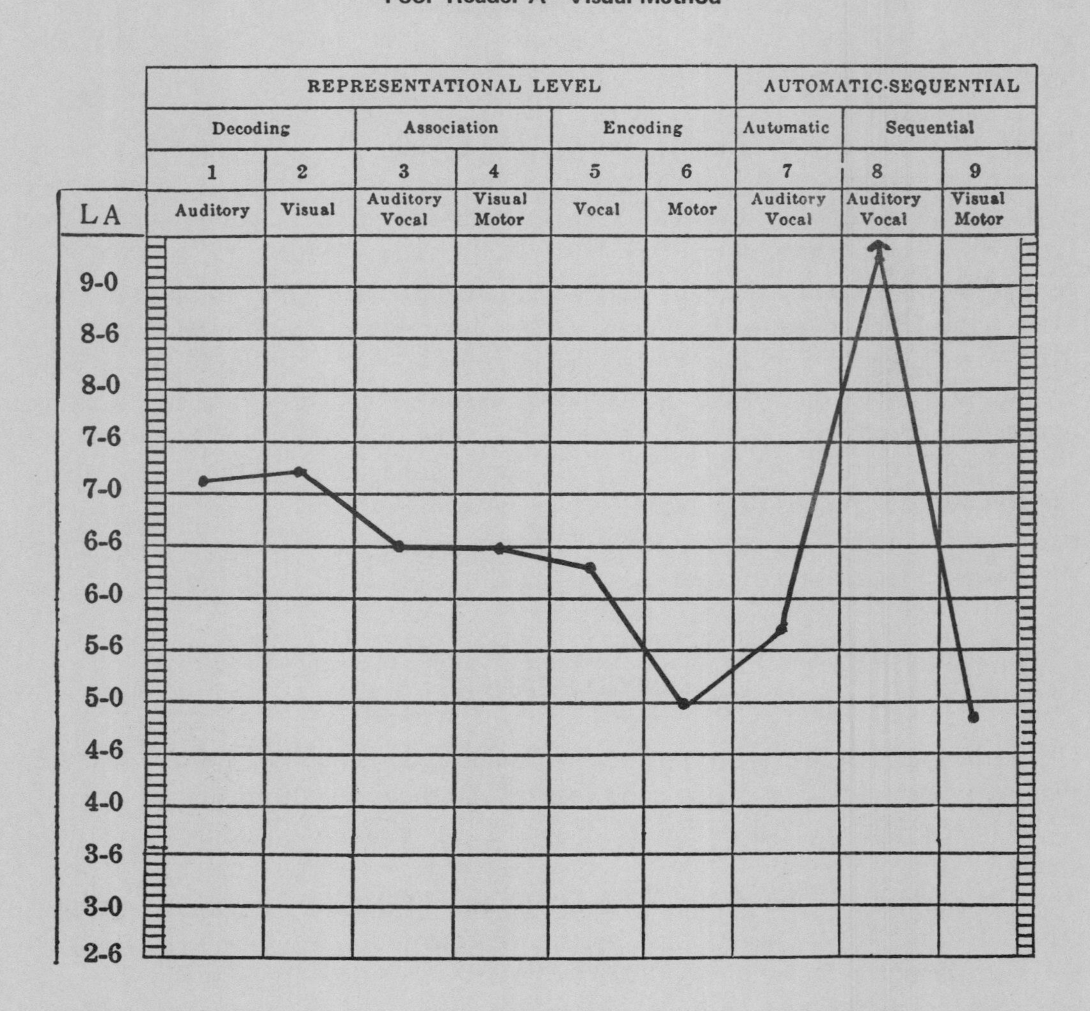

FIGURE 18

Poor Reader B - Visual Method

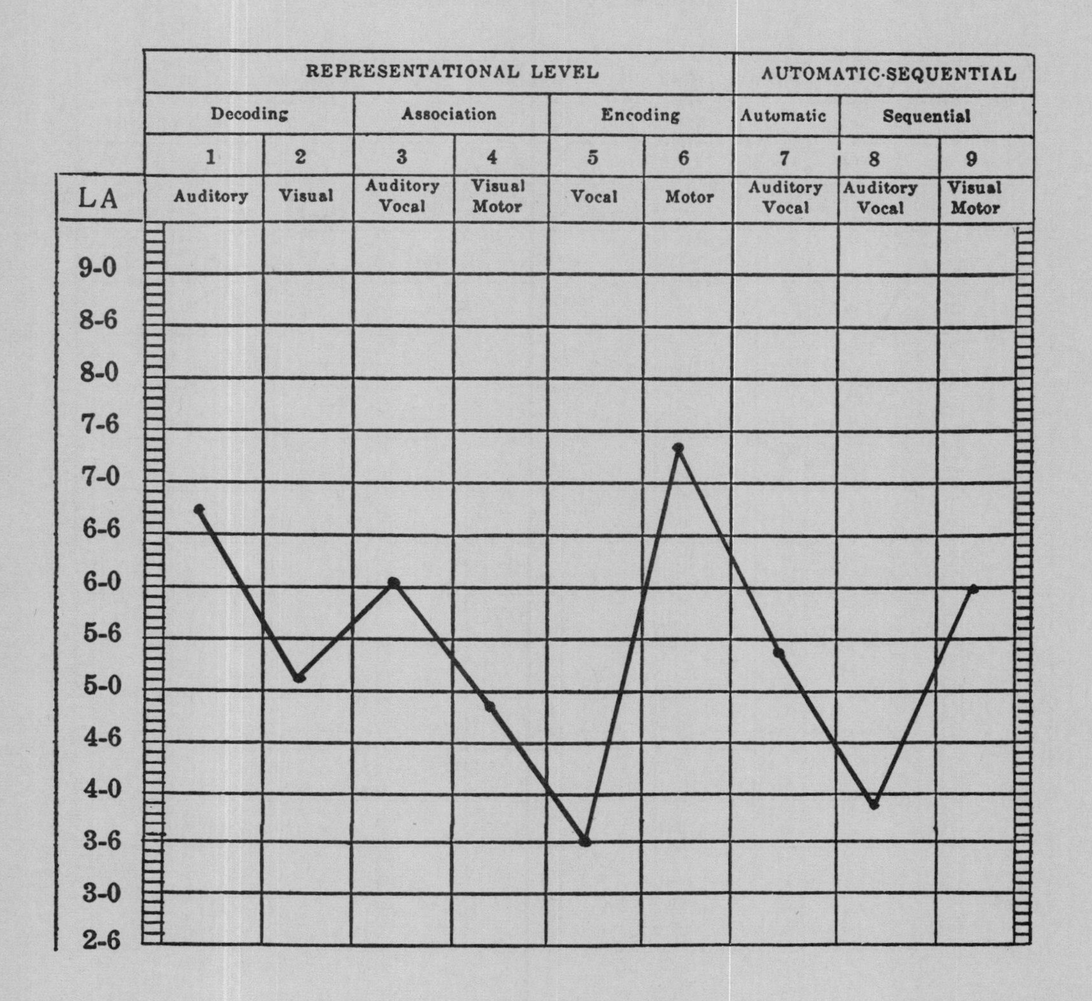

FIGURE 19

Good Reader A - Auditory Method

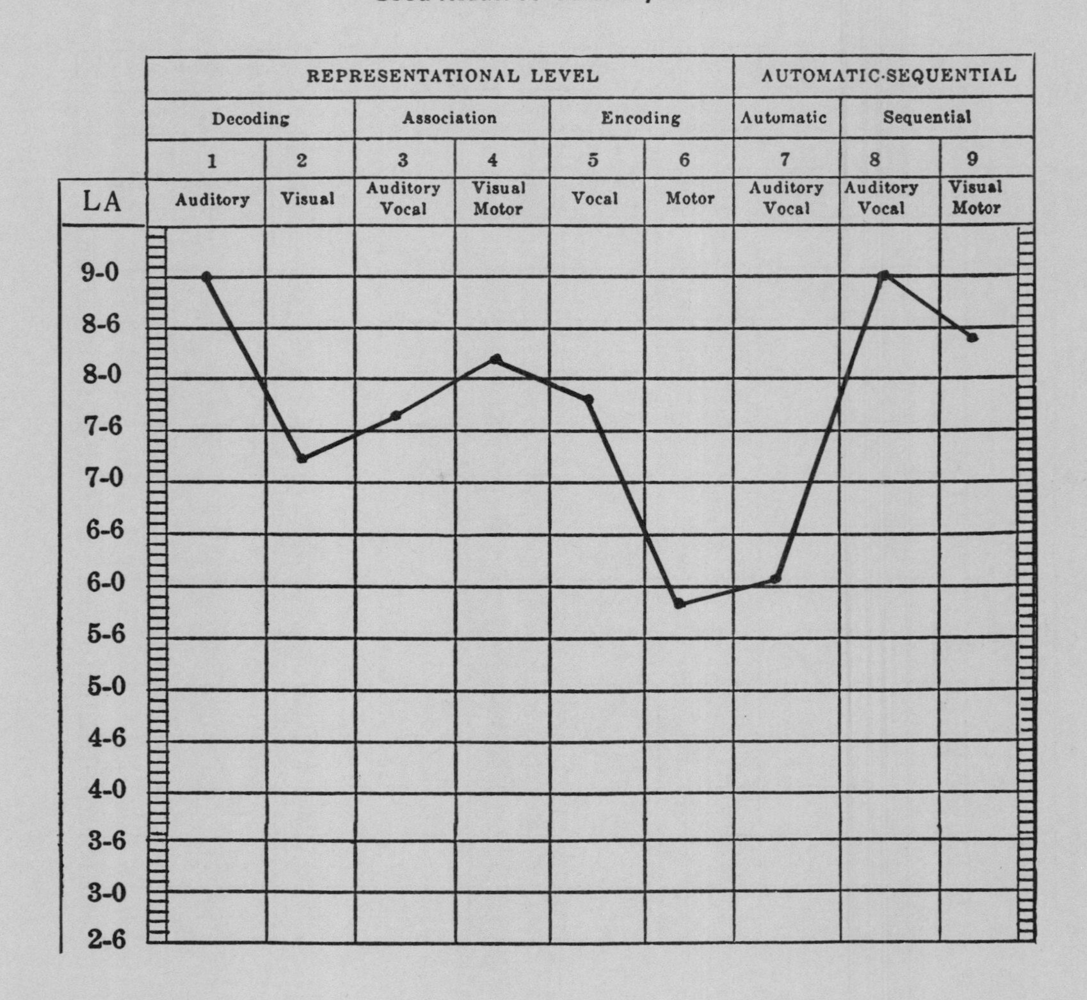

FIGURE 20

Good Reader B - Auditory Method

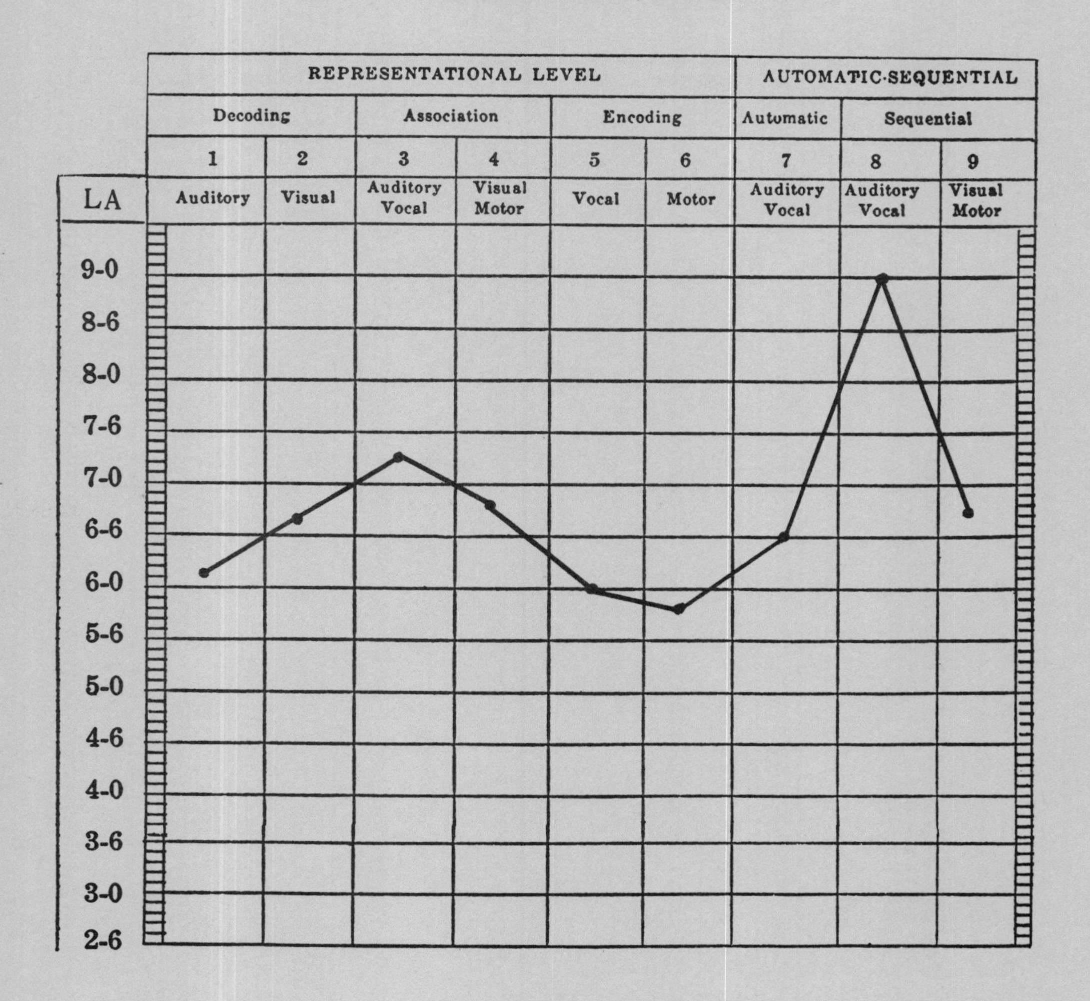

FIGURE 21

Good Reader C - Auditory Method

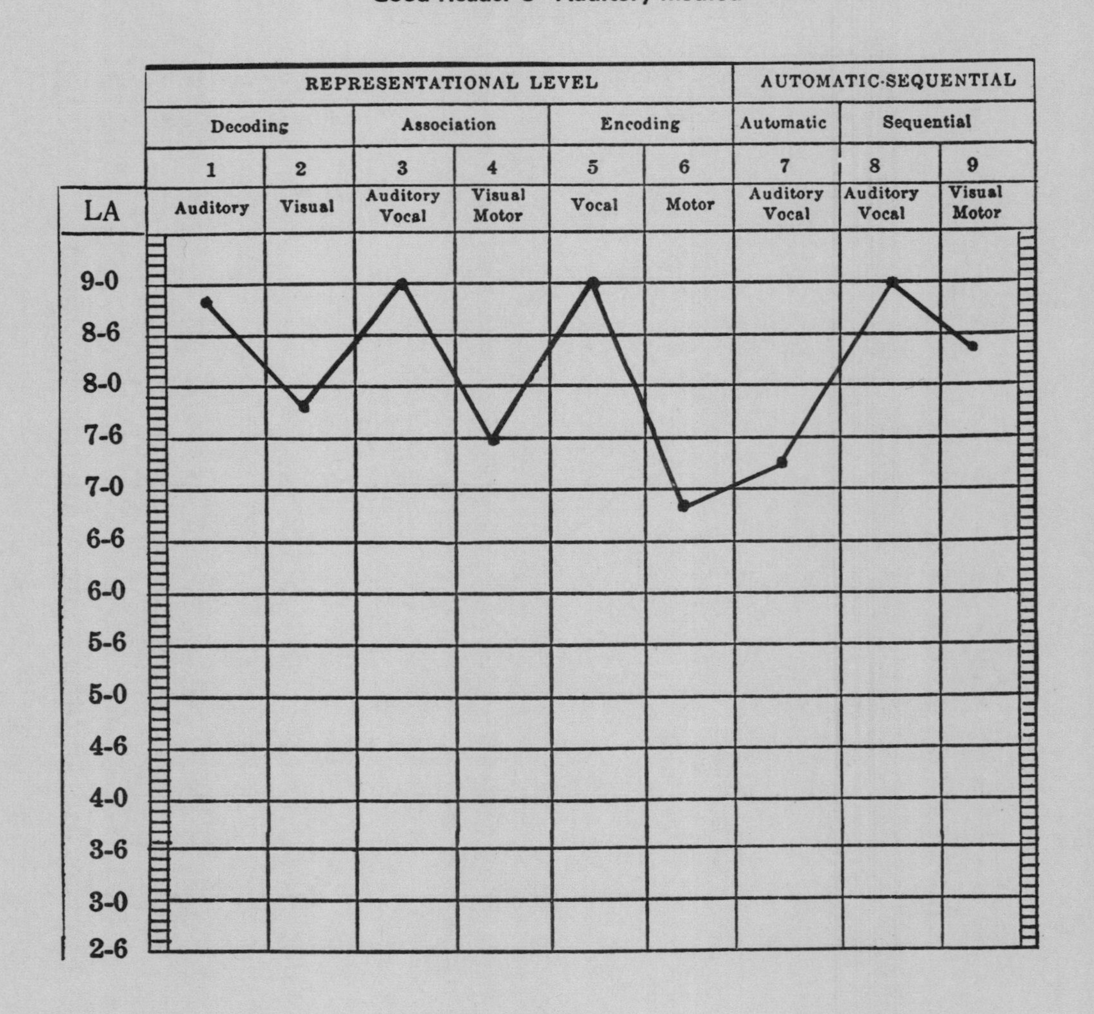

TENTATIVE GENERALIZATIONS

The clinical and research data available on reading and the ITPA suggest the following tentative generalizations:

1. Children with severe and persistent reading disabilities show deficits in both auditory and visual memory. The use in many clinical, remedial programs of a tactual-kinesthetic teaching method is probably a direct result of dual memory deficit and is an implicit gamble that such a child may have better tactual-kinesthetic memory.
2. The child who has poor auditory memory but good visual memory may do reasonably well in the early stages of a visual (sight-word) method of reading instruction, but he will probably run into difficulty when he is expected to develop independent word attack skills and can do longer memorize every new word form (often about third grade). He will probably meet early failure in a phonics method.
3. The child with poor visual memory and good auditory memory may have some difficulty if he is initially taught by a visual method. As soon as phonics are presented, however, his chances of success are excellent, provided he was not totally demoralized by his experience with the sight method. He may well be the child commonly referred to as a "late bloomer". If his initial instruction is in phonics, no difficulties in reading would be expected.
4. Auditory memory seems to be clearly the most important psycholinguistic ability measured by the ITPA, in terms of its role in reading. Visual memory appears somewhat less important in the final analysis.

CHAPTER 4

INTERPRETATION OF INDIVIDUAL ITPA PROFILES

Theoretically we might expect patterns of deficiencies in profiles to correspond to the three dimensions of language postulated in the model of the ITPA and to a large extent, this does occur. Among the most frequent disabilities are channel problems.

VISUAL-MOTOR CHANNEL DISABILITIES

A severe deficiency in all visual-motor subtests would in all probability be related to visual defects. However, even in testing legally blind children a total channel incapacity has not been frequently observed. Figure 22 is the profile of an 8-year-old boy with severe vision problems—cataracts and nystagmus—whose Binet IQ was 109. But even in this case it should be noted that visual memory is intact. The visual discriminations required in this subtest are well within the visual abilities of most partially seeing and a few legally blind youngsters. The ITPA is not intended to be a vision screening test and should not be used that way. Gross visual impairment is necessary to hinder performance and the examiner would in all probability be aware of such extreme difficulty. Complete visual-motor channel incapacitation is extraordinarily rare and the examiner must be prepared to deal with less clear-cut patterns.

One of the most frequently encountered visual-motor disabilities is that shown by the child with the Strauss Syndrome of visual-perceptual problems, hyperactivity, etc. Two of these profiles, both clearly showing the highly characteristic deficiencies in visual decoding and motor encoding are presented in Figure 23.

FIGURE 22

Severe Vision Problem

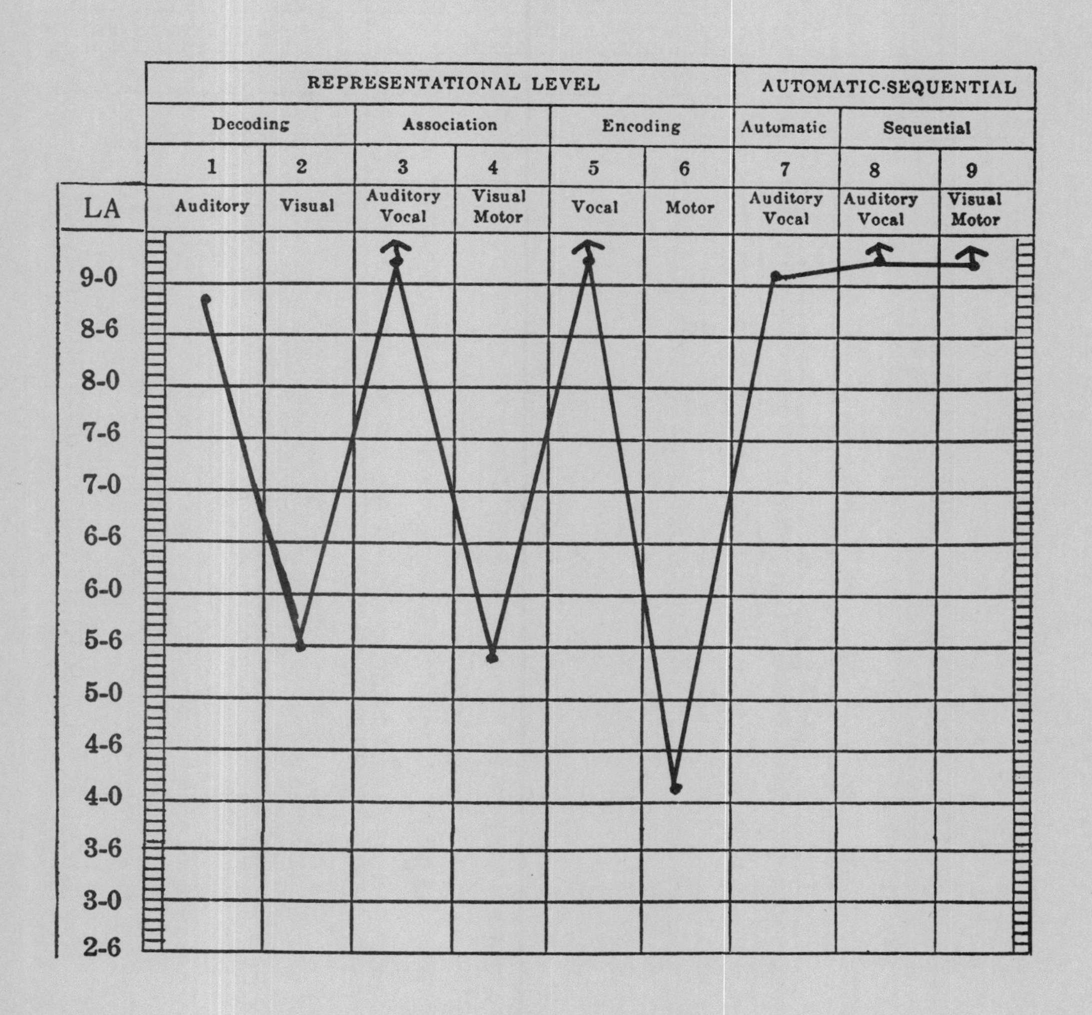

CA: 8-8
IQ: 109

Reference: Bateman, 1963.

FIGURE 23

Two Strauss Syndrome Children

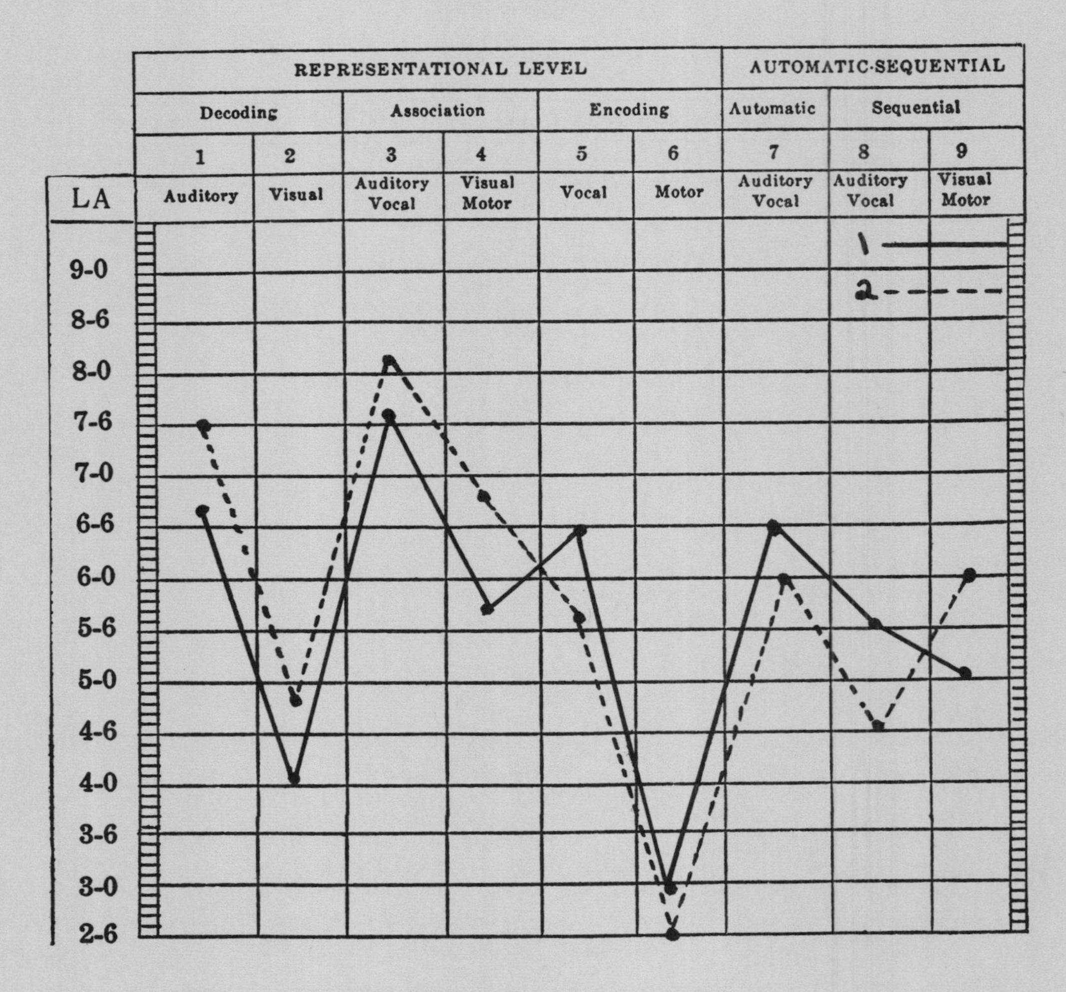

Child 1

CA: 9-9
IQ: 65

Child 2

CA: 6-6
IQ: 90

Reference: Bateman & Wetherell, 1965.

Often very careful clinical judgment is required to evaluate the scores these Strauss Syndrome youngsters obtain on the two sequential subtests. Spuriously or unreliably low scores on the sequential tests frequently accompany distractibility and attentional problems. Auditory-vocal automatic scores for these youngsters seem to be particularly sensitive indices of home background, parental pressure, and verbal intelligence. Interestingly, visual-motor association does not seem to be necessarily affected (although it *may* be) in this basic visual decoding-motor encoding problem.

One extremely important caution must be heeded in looking at a Strauss Syndrome profile. It is identical in shape to that shown by the highly intelligent, very verbal child from achievement-oriented, upper middle class suburbia. In one affluent school, well over half the kindergarten population showed this pattern. After discarding the hasty hypothesis that so-called "minimal brain damage" was contagious and rampant in the community, it was realized that the crucial difference between the Strauss Syndrome profile and the highly verbal profile lies in the level of the profile in relation to the child's CA. In the Strauss Syndrome, visual decoding and motor encoding constitute areas of severe deficiency which are notably below CA; in the highly verbal child, the auditory-vocal scores constitute strengths appreciably above CA and the relatively weaker visual-motor tests are at or only slightly below CA.

When a genuine visual decoding-motor encoding problem is found, further testing should be undertaken to specify the types of remediation necessary and the level at which to begin. Sources like Kephart and Frostig are invaluable in diagnosing this type of deficiency.

Teachers frequently describe these youngsters as immature, flighty, or poorly coordinated children who won't sit still, have short attention spans, etc. Their visual-motor difficulties might show up in handwriting, placement of arithmetic problems on the page, drawings of human or geometric figures, etc.

A motor encoding deficiency which appears together with intact visual decoding is sometimes seen in very shy children. It may not always be necessary or helpful to distinguish between a pure motor encoding disability and a factor of inhibition. In either case, the child does not use his body effectively in conveying meaning.

FIGURE 24

Mentally Retarded 10 year old with Motor Encoding Disability

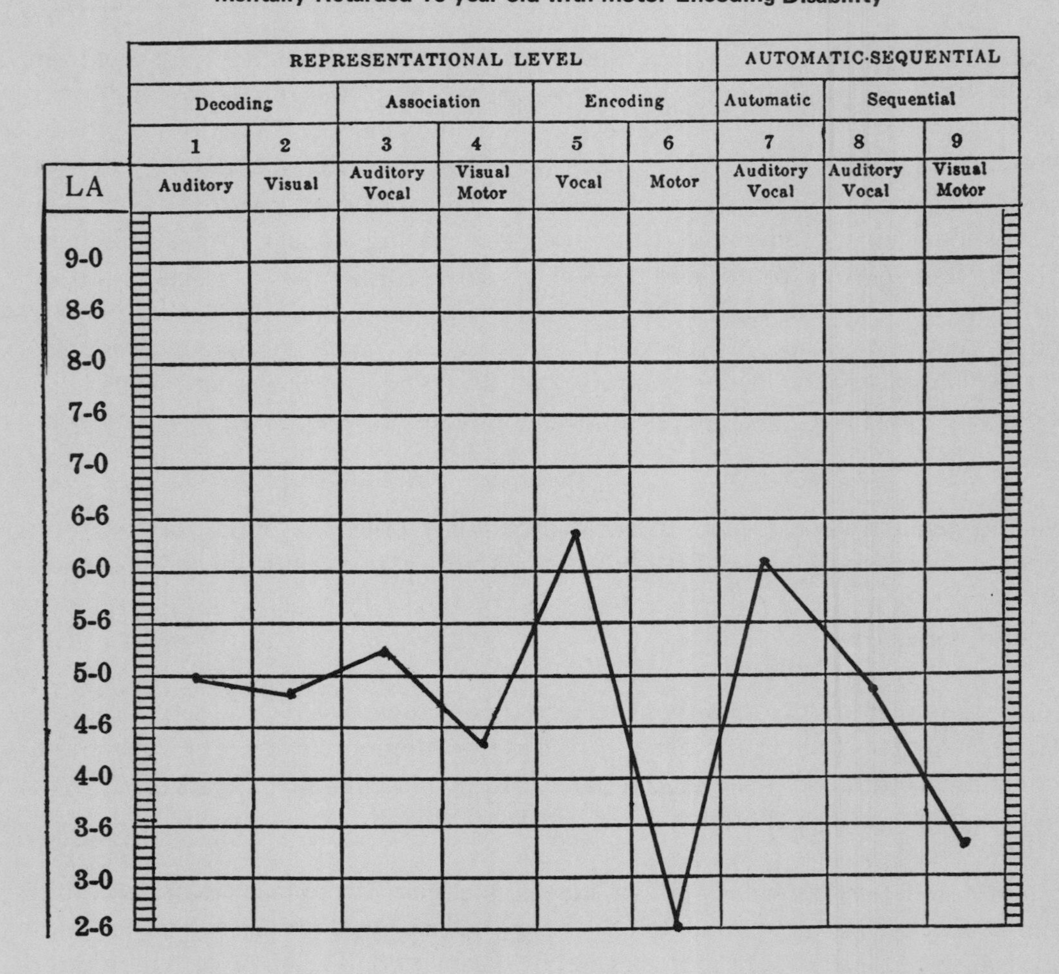

FIGURE 25

"Pseudo" Strauss Syndrome in a Shy 8 year old Girl

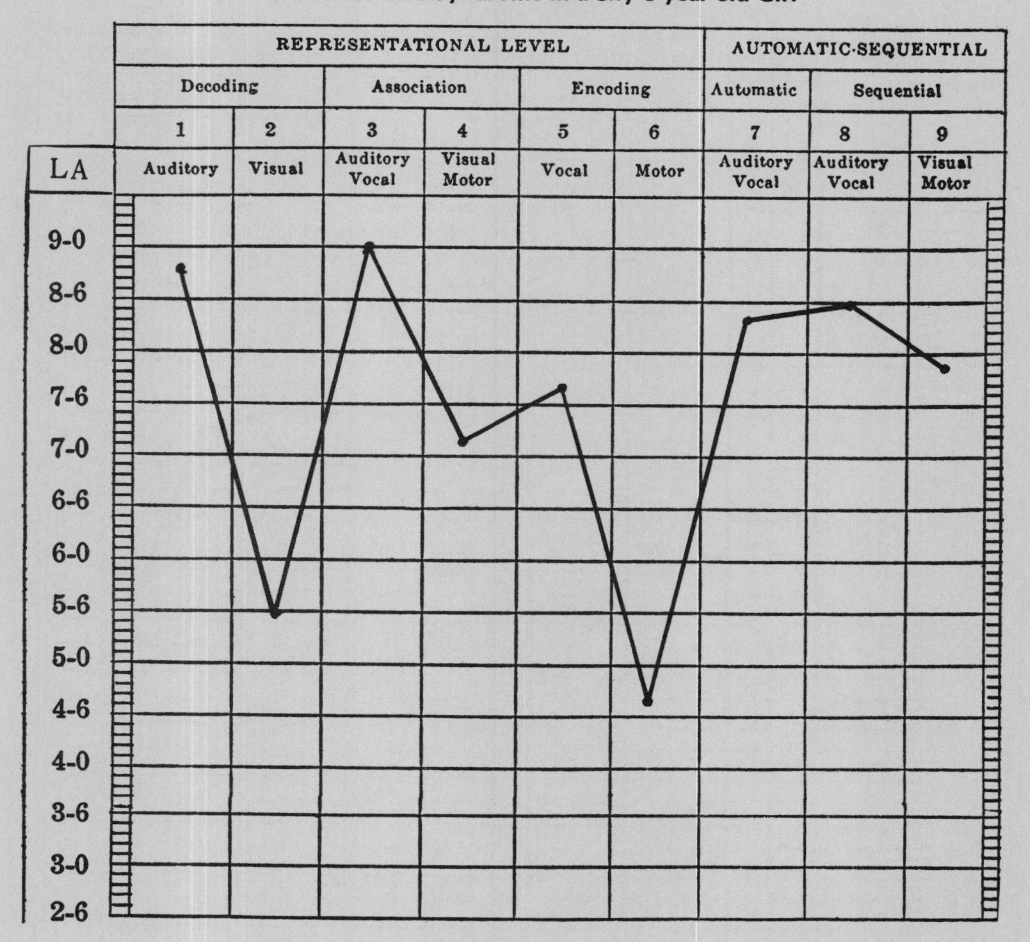

FIGURE 26

Effeminate 10 year old retarded male

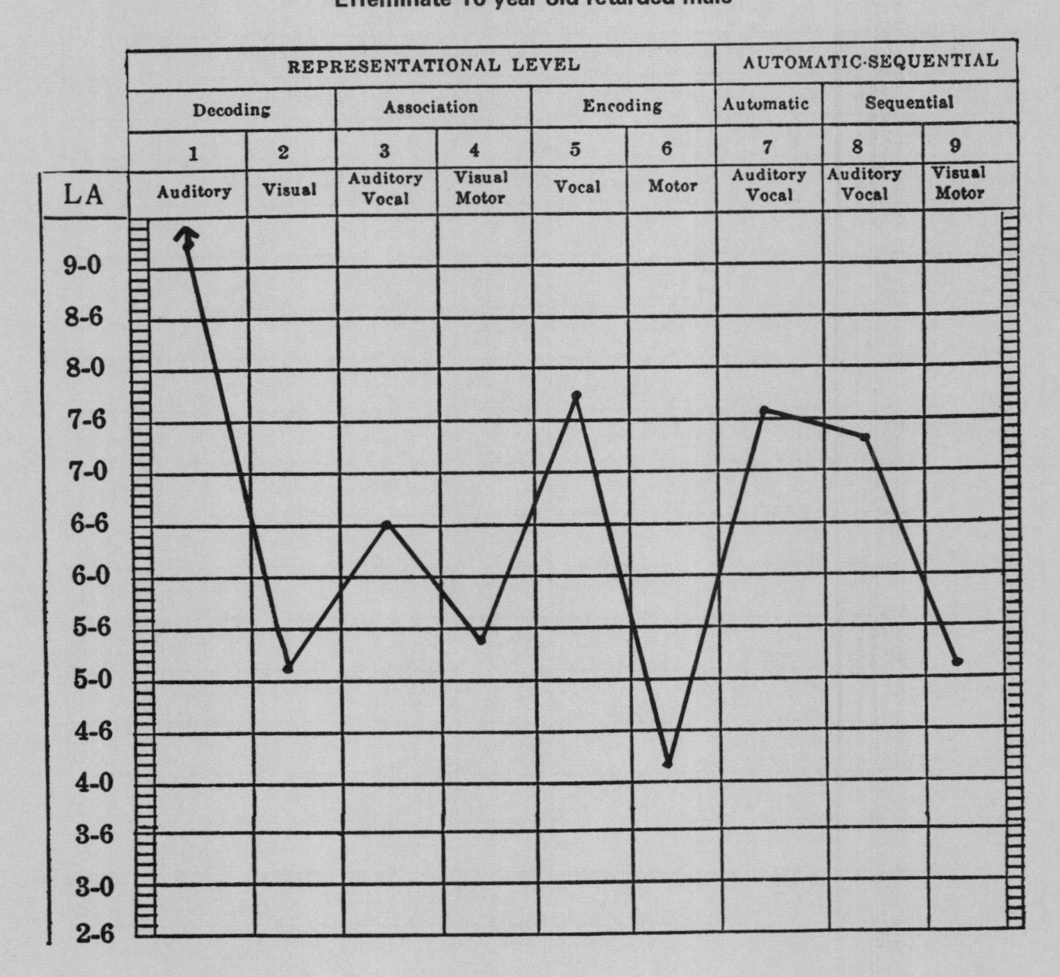

Deficiencies in visual-motor association must be interpreted quite cautiously since the reliability of the visual-motor subtests, particularly this one, is somewhat lower than that of the auditory-vocal tests. A deficiency is sometimes seen in visual-motor association which is consistent with and supportive of a fairly general visual-motor deficiency. But when visual-motor association is the only subtest on this channel which is down, one might well suspect something else. In one case, a child had such a severe linguistic auditory-vocal problem that he could not consistently process the concept "goes with". Much more common is the youngster who chooses wrong responses for excellent reasons. The examiner must keep in mind that on both visual-motor association and visual decoding the correct response was originally determined by the majority answers of the standardization subjects.

Figures 24-26 are profiles of individual children who showed variations of visual-motor problems. The mentally retarded child in Figure 24 shows a severe motor encoding without a visual decoding deficit. This by itself is unusual, as is the severity of the deficiency. His performance on motor encoding was subjectively described on the protocol as "weird." He gave unusual and bizarre responses such as putting the drill to his ear, waving one finger in the air for the safe, choking himself with the stethoscope, and holding both hands above his head for the violin. His motor coordination was excellent. These observations combined with the strong auditory-vocal automatic (which is unusual for retardates) might suggest an emotional disorder.

The girl in Figure 25 was described by the examiner as easily inhibited, self-effacing, cooperative, passive and in need of much encouragement. Frequently, girls of 7 to 9 years of age are particularly constrained in their motor encoding performance. Blind profile analysis alone cannot always differentiate this kind of performance from the hyperactive Strauss Syndrome child, but in this case the good performance in both memory tests is a strong clue that the child was not distractible and did have a good attention span.

Figure 26 shows a mildly mentally handicapped boy who can best be described as extraordinarily effeminate. His clothes are always immaculate, he appears to move only his ankles, wrists, and eyes when he walks, he always speaks in a most precise and highly inflected manner. It has been frequently suggested that the goal of remediation should be to involve him in a fight on a muddy playground.

AUDITORY-VOCAL CHANNEL DISABILITIES

A non-speaking, deaf child would not be expected to score on the auditory-vocal subtests at all. A severely "aphasic" child would show a highly similar profile; although one might not be surprised to see some scoring on auditory decoding or on auditory-vocal sequential. These total channel problems are relatively rare, however, just as are total visual-motor problems.

Auditory decoding often requires somewhat more interpretation than do the other auditory-vocal tests. A spuriously high score can be obtained by the child who is able to guess well above the chance level, perhaps by picking up minimal examiner cues such as inflections. On the other hand, a spuriously low score can be obtained by the child who is reading too much into the questions, but fails to reveal this. For example, a very bright child once answered "no" to "Do microscopes magnify?" When queried about this later, he explained that the lens does the magnifying. It is especially important on this subtest to cross check his score with his daily behavior. It is difficult to work individually with a youngster for an hour without making a clinical assessment of his ability to understand what is said to him. Occasionally a child is quite able to understand the auditory decoding items, all of which are three word questions having the same structure (Do X's y?), and still be unable to follow ordinary conversation or directions.

Auditory-vocal association is notable in at least two ways. First, it correlates remarkably well with Binet MA (.93 - .97), although it frequently underestimates Binet MA by 5 to 10%. This seems to be especially true for mentally retarded children who accumulate many months of mental age on the predominantly visual-motor subtests of the Binet below year VII. Since retarded children as a group function better on the visual-motor than on the auditory-vocal channel, the difference in weighting of the two channels on the Binet above and below age 7, operates to consistently show MA higher than auditory-vocal association.

The relationship between auditory-vocal association and vocal encoding may be very revealing. Many youngsters have been seen whose ability to give very short verbal answers to highly structured questions (such as presented in auditory-vocal association and auditory-vocal automatic) is quite intact, but whose relatively spontaneous and unstructured verbal output is grossly limited. The opposite is also possible in which vocal encoding may be quite high (but often circuitous and imprecise) but the more specific answers quite deviant. This latter type of performance frequently results in the youngster being described as "brighter than the tests show," just because encoding behavior is readily visible to the casual observer. When motor encoding is also high a very misleading image can be created. Figure 27 is the profile of a youngster whose very high motor and vocal encoding abilities do give him the appearance of being much brighter than he is. He is actually mentally retarded and very small for his age; but he is often thought by casual observers to be normal.

Figure 28 shows a five-year-old girl who, on global tests of intelligence,scores in the mentally retarded range. But the ITPA reveals she is normal on the visual-motor channel and grossly deficient in the auditory-vocal area. Vocal encoding appears, on the surface, to be the basic deficiency which accounts for the other areas of weakness. But in cases similar to this it has been found after remediation that auditory-vocal automatic or incidental verbal learning may be the primary deficit.

Figures 29 and 30 both show mentally retarded children who also have learning disorders calling for remediation in the auditory-vocal channel. Figure 32, while also revealing a slight auditory-vocal disability, depicts a typical profile for a retardate. This slight weakness in the auditory-vocal area is expected for retardates and does not constitute a learning disorder.

Vocal encoding deficiencies must be viewed in the light of the scoring which takes only quantity, not quality of verbal response into account. This subtest, like auditory decoding, is relatively easy to check against personal observation of how well the youngster is able to express ideas verbally. If he expresses himself well outside the testing situation, but scores poorly, an explanation other than a genuine vocal encoding deficiency must be sought.

FIGURE 27

High Encoding in an 8 year old Retarded Male

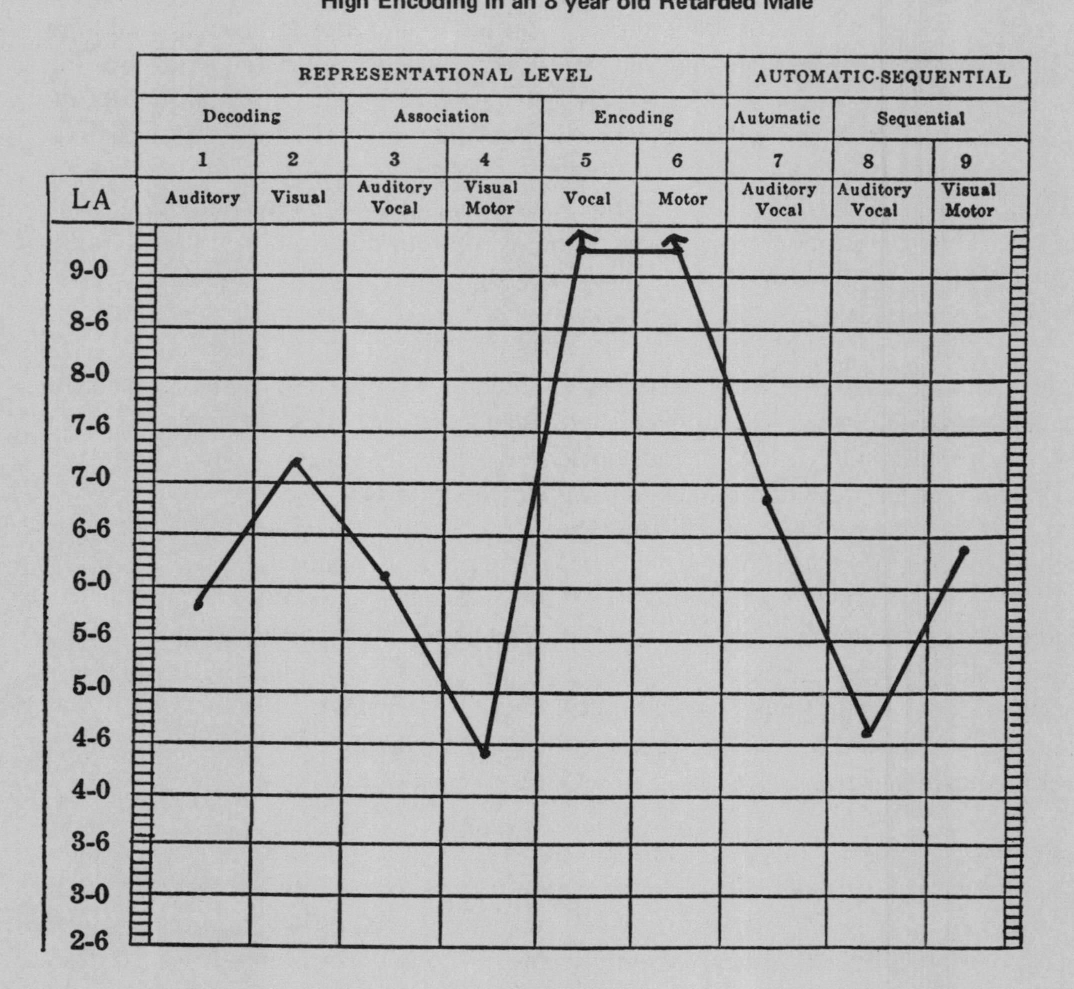

FIGURE 28

Severe Auditory-Vocal Channel Deficit
in a 5 year old Female

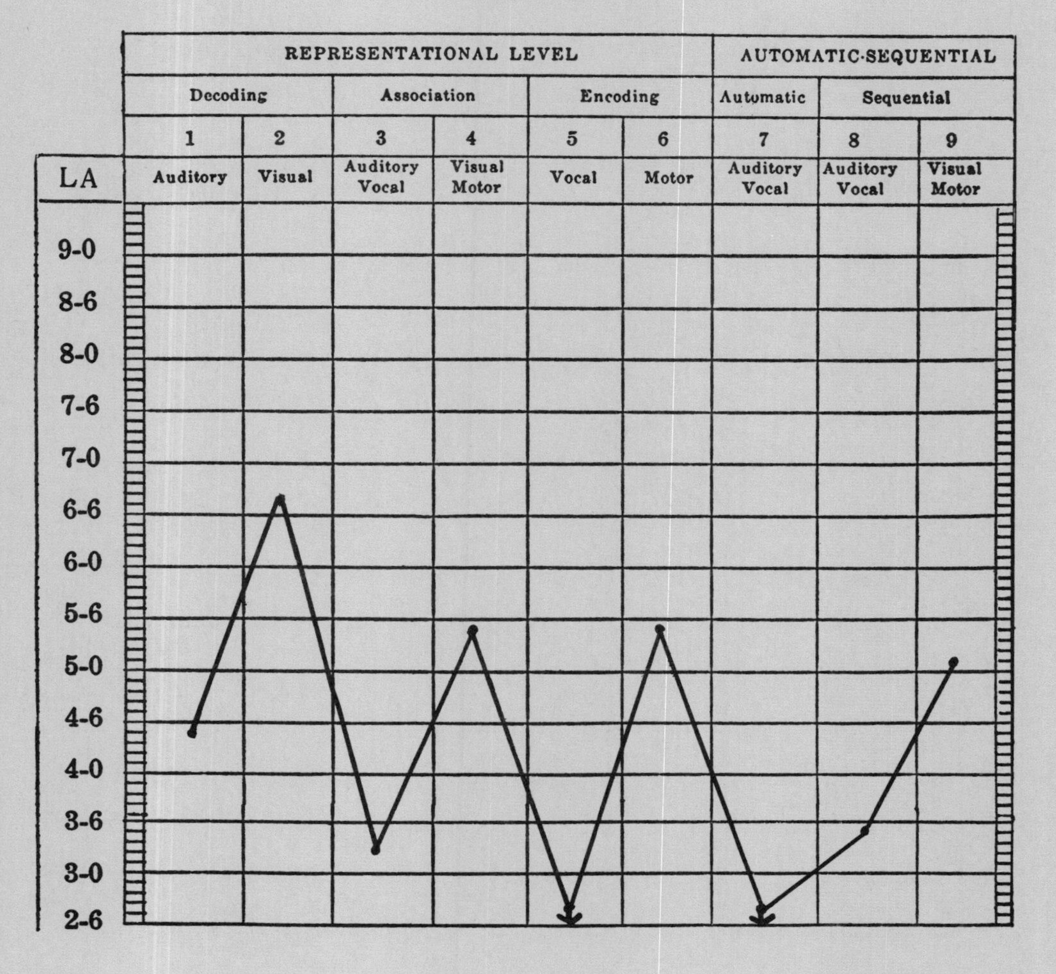

FIGURE 29

Retarded 9 year old with Auditory-Vocal Channel Deficit

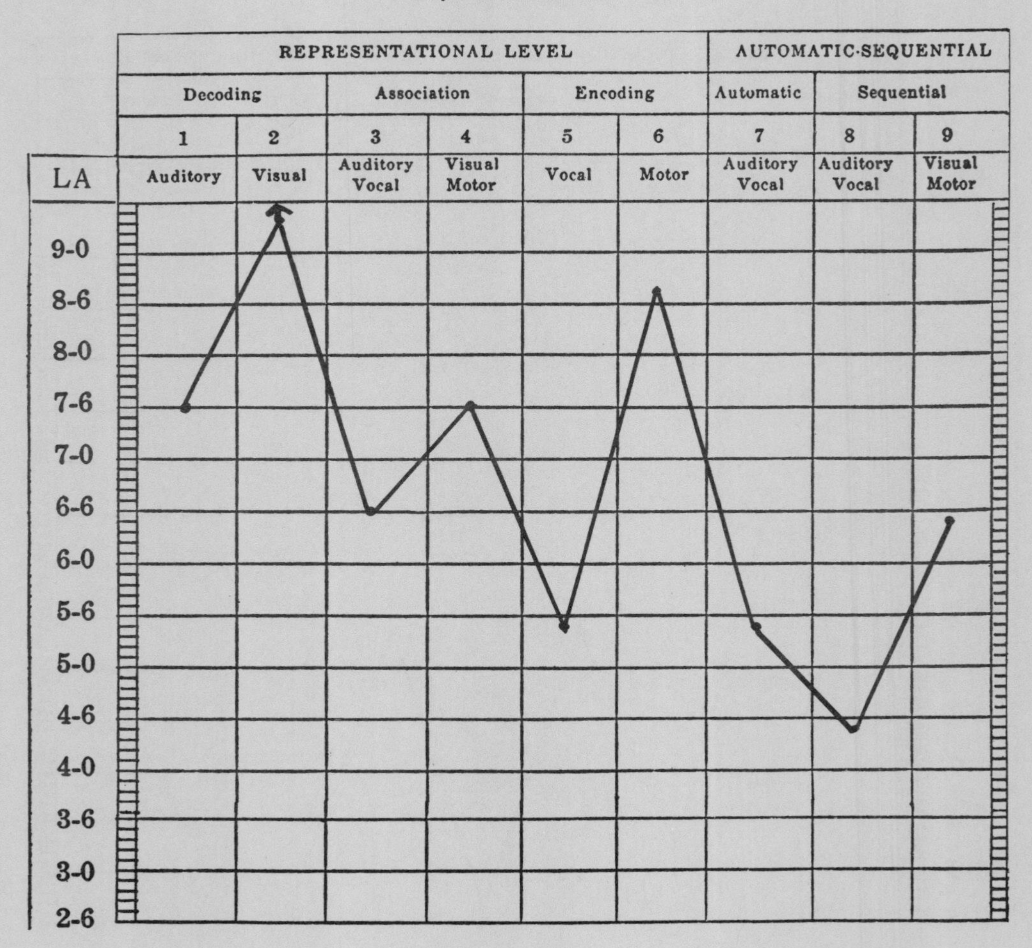

FIGURE 30

Retarded 10 year old with Auditory-Vocal Channel Deficit

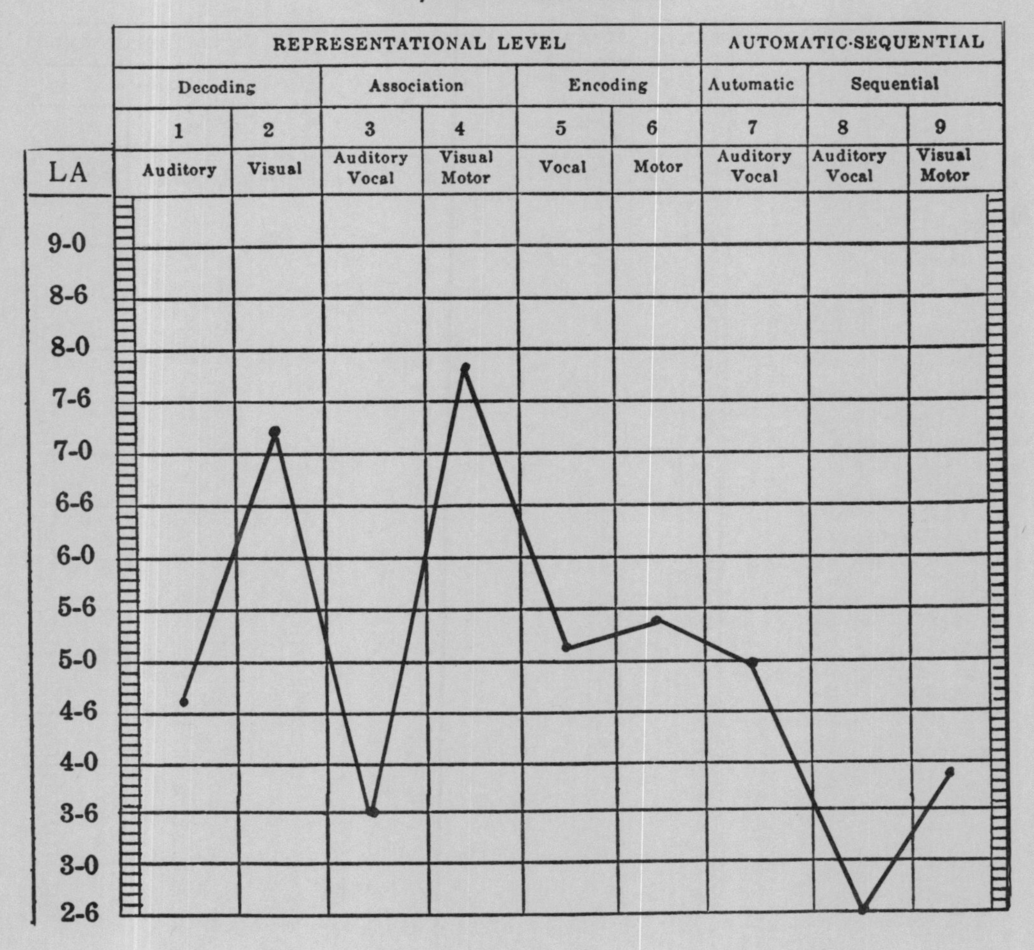

FIGURE 31

Retarded Child with Typical Auditory-Vocal Channel Performance

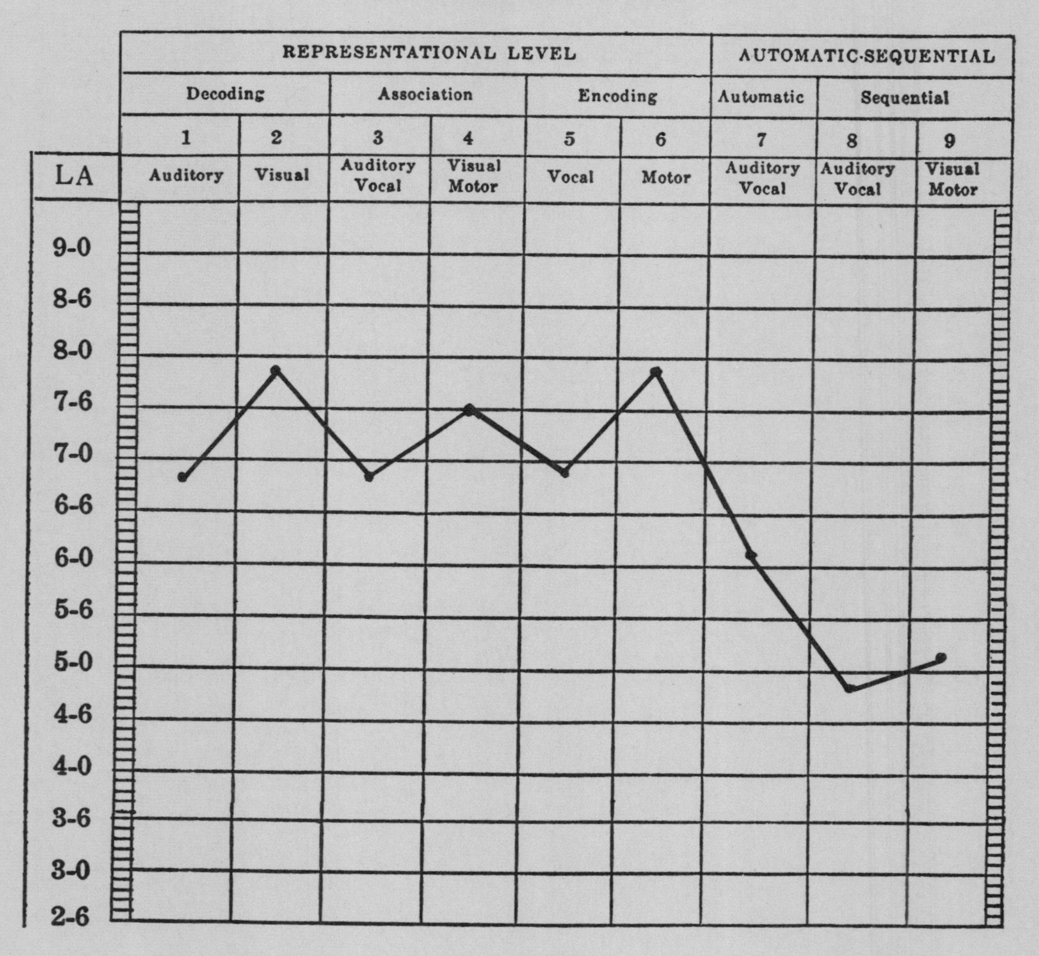

DETAILED INTERPRETATION OF ONE PROFILE

The following slightly edited transcript of the writer's in-class discussion of the profile (Fig. 32) of a youngster who showed an auditory-vocal channel problem is presented in the hope that the detailed analysis of this case will reveal the kinds of considerations that enter into profile analysis involving the auditory-vocal channel. The ITPA was administered to the subject as a demonstration test in the same room with 40 psychology students. The subject and examiner had not previously met and no information other than CA was available to the examiner, except as it was revealed by the subject's language therapist during the subsequent discussion.

Because this ITPA was given under these circumstances, it obviously cannot be considered a valid clinical test. But for the sake of discussion it will be treated as such.

FIGURE 32

David (CA=9-0)

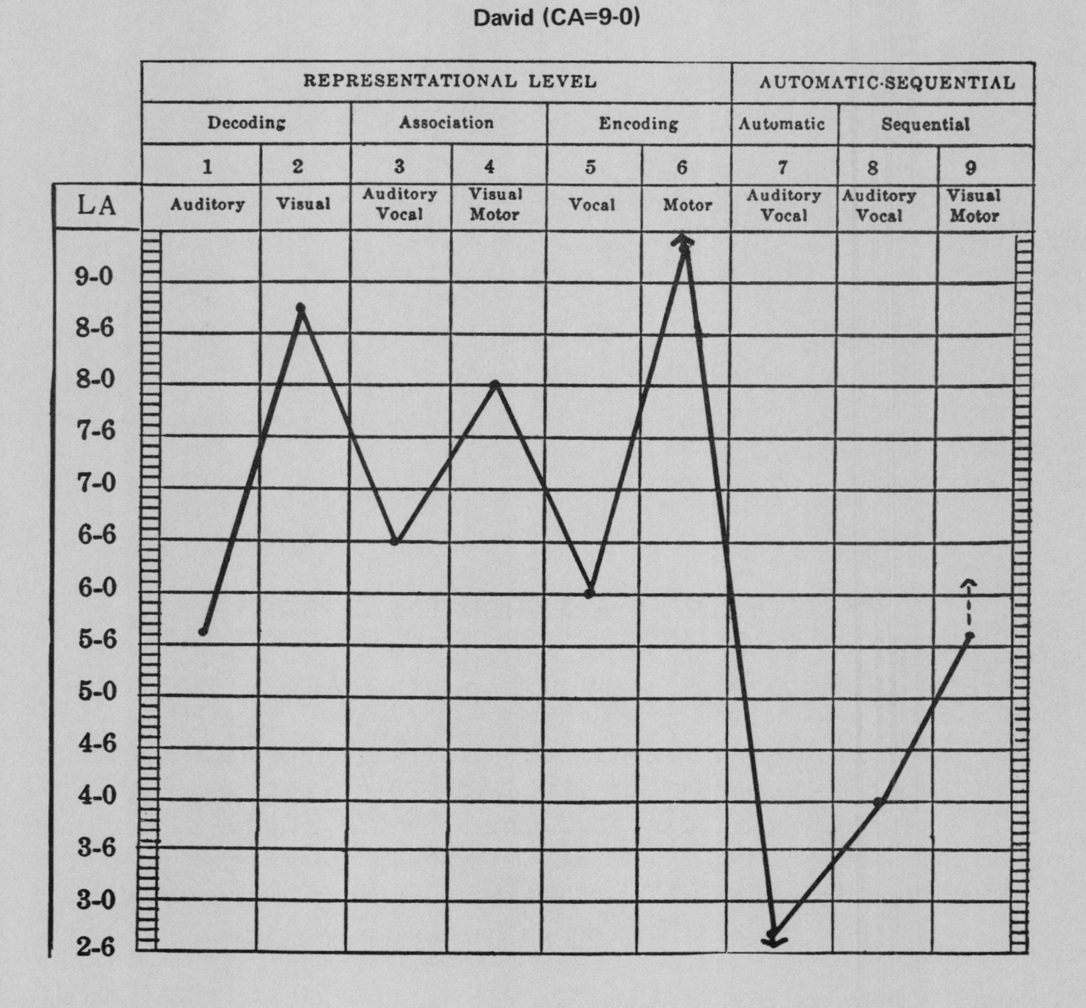

In each case David's visual-motor performance was higher than his corresponding auditory-vocal performance. On visual decoding he was three years higher than on auditory decoding. He was a year and a half higher on visual-motor than on auditory-vocal association. In general, he is operating about three years higher on the visual-motor than on the auditory-vocal channel, at the representational level. The very high performance on motor encoding could have been predicted on the basis that this youngster does not operate effectively on his auditory-vocal channel--whether he is hard of hearing or disturbed or what--we don't know. But for youngsters who do not efficiently receive or express information on the auditory channel we predict very high motor encoding and he had it.

At the automatic-sequential level, dealing with the nonmeaningful aspects of language, we find that he is below norms on auditory-vocal automatic (grammar). It is highly unusual for the same youngster to be above norms on one subtest and below norms on another. This is the kind of thing that Kirk is talking about when he speaks about real discrepancies within the child, when he operates like a 9-or 10-year-old in one way and like a 2-or 3-year-old in another way. It appears that auditory memory is a genuine disability and in fact a very basic problem; if I were doing an individual diagnosis, I'd certainly pursue it further. I'd not accept this one sample of digit span behavior. The visual memory test was stopped before the ceiling was reached so this is a very minimal estimate. He does appear to have some difficulty in visual memory, but it's not nearly as extreme as his auditory memory problem. Again we see the consistent preference for the visual channel over the auditory-vocal channel.

David scored 6-6 on auditory-vocal association which, since he is chronologically 9-1, suggests an IQ of about 70, [language therapist volunteers he scored exactly 70 on his last Binet.] So he is operating at an EMH level. Mentally retarded children are characterized, above all, by a discrepancy between the representational level and the automatic-sequential level. He looks like a typical mentally retarded child with respect to this finding, with the representational level ranging from the 6 to 9 year level range and his automatic-sequential level from the 2 to 5 year level. His profile also looks like that of a culturally deprived youngster, although he did not give the appearance of being culturally deprived. But the very high motor encoding and the very low grammar do suggest that. If one saw just the profile and knew nothing else, one would say EMH, culturally deprived with an auditory-vocal channel problem. [Member of the audience volunteers information that he is severely culturally deprived.] Since he is culturally deprived, we hit it right on the head on all three major points . . . . .

On auditory-vocal automatic you noticed that I first tested to see if the "s" sound was present. If a youngster doesn't have an "s" sound, he is not penalized for failure to make the proper plural. In other words, we're not interested in testing articulation--we're testing grammar, so if he doesn't have an "s" you prorate credit. He had an "s" but he did not use it to form plurals, as culturally deprived youngsters often don't.

David handled visual decoding in a very mature, intelligent way. He was actually figuring out--he was not guessing. His score of 8-9 is almost at the top of the norms, so all we know for sure is that he does not have a problem there.

He handled motor encoding very well. His movements were extremely precise--one of the highest levels of motor encoding performance that you ever expect to see. The only items for which he failed to get full credit were the violin, which he perceived as a guitar, and the saw where he could have received an extra point had he held the board with one hand while he was sawing with the other hand. Other than that, it was a perfect performance.

On auditory-vocal association--"soup is hot, ice cream is   "--his performance was surprisingly good. Surprisingly in that, up to this point, I hadn't had much idea of how strong his auditory-vocal channel was. He had gotten only one point on the other auditory-vocal tests and then he came through at this 6-6 level which was pretty good. I made a mistake in judgment on this subtest. On item # 17--"a man may be a king, a woman may be a   "--his response was not intelligible to me and I violated a very important general principle which is: "never to ask a child to repeat unless you absolutely have to," because of just exactly what happened. He thought I was saying in effect that his response had been wrong and he came out with "wife." Initially I had not been able to tell whether he was saying "king" or "queen" and knowing that many children when they begin to break down and can't do any more of the opposite analogies, tend to repeat the last word of the phrase that you have given them, I was afraid that if he were saying "king." ("A man may be a king, a woman may be a **king.**") *he would persist in this pattern throughout the rest of the test. A lot of things went through my mind and I weighed my desire for him not to start an erroneous pattern, and I guessed wrong. It did upset him. We try very hard to train our testers to hear things the first time so they don't have to ask for repetition because this does happen very frequently.*

On visual-motor sequencing, I couldn't tell whether he was beginning to make mistakes and goof around because he was reaching his ceiling or whether he was genuinely having trouble because he was tired. And you (directed to the member of the audience who had been working with David) said before you were surprised that he stayed as close to being awake as he did. Well, he had not actually reached a ceiling on visual memory. He had missed only two items, but I felt at that point we had to go on because I didn't want to lose him. The 5-8 is therefore a minimum estimate and I just don't know whether he could have done more or not. If he is in fact operating at a Binet mental age of about 6-6, then we did establish that this is not a severe deficit for him.

The vocal encoding was surprising in that we had heard that he was basically quite non-verbal and for him to come out at the 6-0 level probably illustrates one of the difficulties in this subtest. We're measuring only quantity of response--not quality. Only once or twice he gave more than just a one-word response to the objects. He did say as he was fanning himself with the plastic, "cool off" and for the ball he said it was "kind of hard," but mainly they were simple one-word responses.

On the auditory memory test he had trouble with three digits and this is with a one-half second interval which is much easier than the Binet one-second interval. While this certainly appeared to be a genuine deficiency it would have to be confirmed by other tests.

The auditory decoding test was bothering some of you. Why didn't I accept his plaintive "don't know" to items like "Do monograms lubricate?" In the standardization procedure, every child was required to answer "yes" or "no" to every item and this guessing factor is built into the norms so that you must do it. If you accept "don't know" you are depriving the child of his 50-50 chance of getting it right. Auditory decoding is something that you're observing as you give the whole test. Does he understand what you say to him? And I was quite satisfied that he did, especially when there were visual cues along with it. For example, in the visual memory when he had the tray out in front of him, he knew immediately that he was to put them back the same way they had been and he didn't get all of this visually. He was also listening and understanding.

David, first of all, is not "really" mentally retarded even though he is clearly operating at about an IQ of 70. We would say that on the basis of his normal, or almost normal, performance on the visual-motor channel and his extreme discrepancies among his own abilities, that he is not a "genuinely" or "typically' or across-the-board mentally retarded child, but rather that he is a child with learning disorders. We would first of all have his hearing checked or check the records to make sure that this is not an acuity problem. I would **not** *ask, as you can verify I* **did not** *ask, anything about his background or whatever happened to him. Right now today for whatever reasons, he is operating like this. After we used other tests, as we always would to verify each of these points, we would say his basic deficiencies are in auditory-vocal automatic and auditory memory. Our diagnosis or our label is that this child suffers from two very basic deficiencies--one in incidental verbal learning, which is grammar, coupled with a severe deficiency in auditory memory. We would therefore begin a language training program in these two areas of grammar and auditory memory after further diagnostic testing in both areas.*

BRIEF COMMENTARY ON INDIVIDUAL PROFILES AND RELIABILITY OF CLINICAL JUDGMENT

In July, 1965, the writer had occasion to hastily view about 100 ITPA profiles of public school kindergarteners who were referred to a research project by their teachers as possibly having potential learning problems. The "blind analysis" comments on some of these profiles were recorded exactly as given below. Five months later, the same profiles were re-examined with no reference to the earlier comments. The second comments were also recorded. In both cases, the basic question being asked was whether the profile indicated learning problems.

These profiles (Fig. 33-42) and unedited comments are presented (1) to give an "undoctored" view of the reliability and lack of reliability of one clinician's views and (2) to provide further glimpses into the kinds of considerations possibly involved in the interpretation of ITPA profiles. Unfortunately, no validity data are available. All children are between 5½ and 6 years of age.

FIGURE 33

K. H.

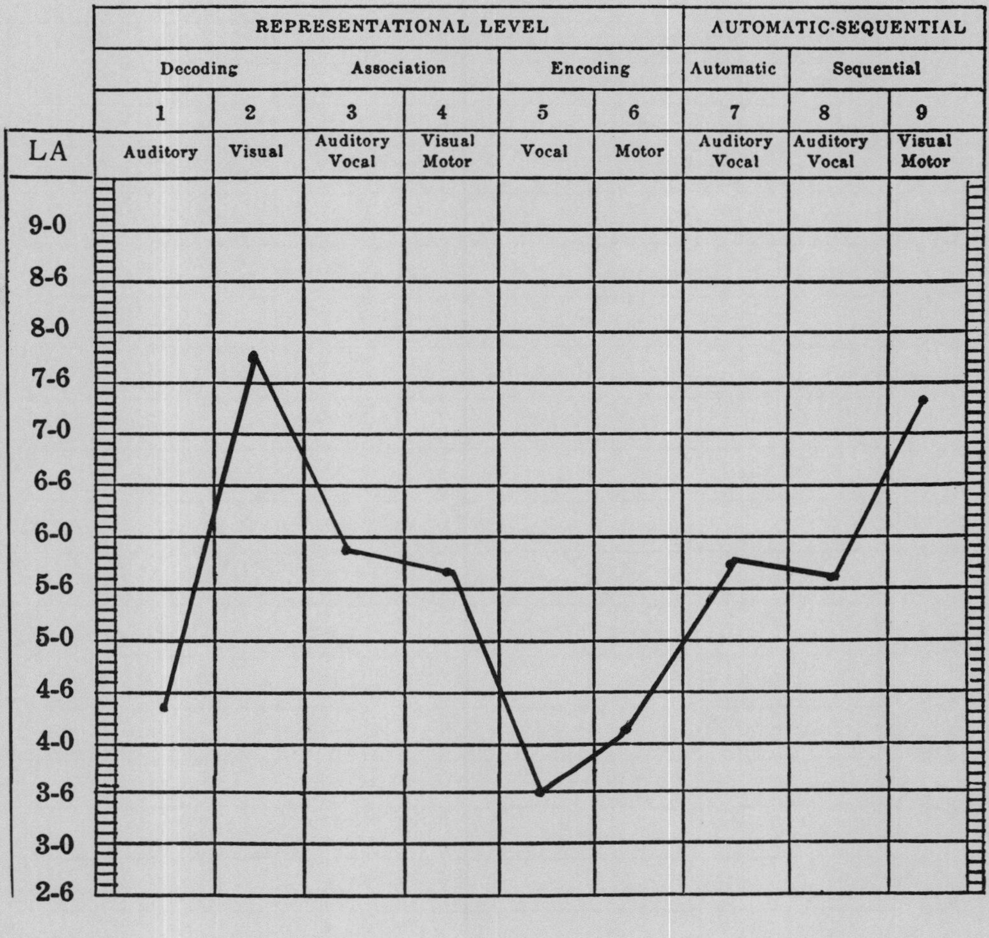

	REPRESENTATIONAL LEVEL						AUTOMATIC-SEQUENTIAL		
	Decoding		Association		Encoding		Automatic	Sequential	
	1	2	3	4	5	6	7	8	9
LA	Auditory	Visual	Auditory Vocal	Visual Motor	Vocal	Motor	Auditory Vocal	Auditory Vocal	Visual Motor
9-0									
8-6									
8-0									
7-6									
7-0									
6-6									
6-0									
5-6									
5-0									
4-6									
4-0									
3-6									
3-0									
2-6									

Additional Information

a. This youngster shows apparent reluctance to express herself. This is fairly consistent on both the vocal and motor encoding. Difficult to tell whether this is a genuine learning disorder or personality factor of inhibition. Appears to have quite good prospects for reading on the basis of the substantial auditory memory and excellent visual memory. Would guess child to be shy but cooperative.

b. Possible encoding problems, but also might be a personality factor. Good visual memory score suggests good attention and desire to please. See a rather passive youngster of average ability. Suspect it is not learning problem and recommend retesting in encoding by someone she knows and likes.

FIGURE 34

D. Z.

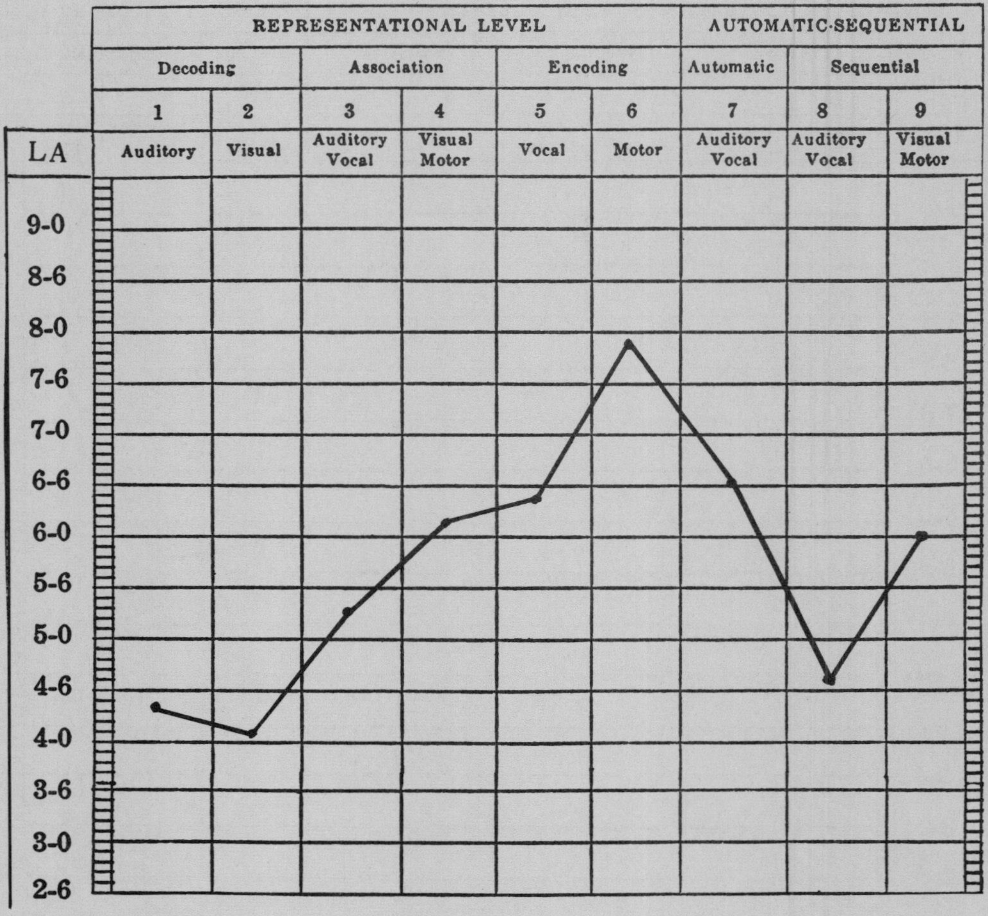

REPRESENTATIONAL LEVEL | AUTOMATIC-SEQUENTIAL

Decoding | Association | Encoding | Automatic | Sequential

LA | 1 Auditory | 2 Visual | 3 Auditory Vocal | 4 Visual Motor | 5 Vocal | 6 Motor | 7 Auditory Vocal | 8 Auditory Vocal | 9 Visual Motor

9-0
8-6
8-0
7-6
7-0
6-6
6-0
5-6
5-0
4-6
4-0
3-6
3-0
2-6

Additional Information

a. Appears to have definite learning problems in the receptive areas. Very high motor encoding in combination with low auditory decoding and auditory memory suggests either a hearing loss in the past or a mild loss at present. Would definitely recommend audiometric check. If hearing acuity is normal would suggest work on receptive language functions and would suggest minimizing motor encoding. Definitely does appear to have either auditory acuity impairment or learning disorder.

b. Low decoding definitely appears to constitute a learning problem. Comes from a "good" home. Problem in auditory memory might suggest poor reading.

FIGURE 35

C. K.

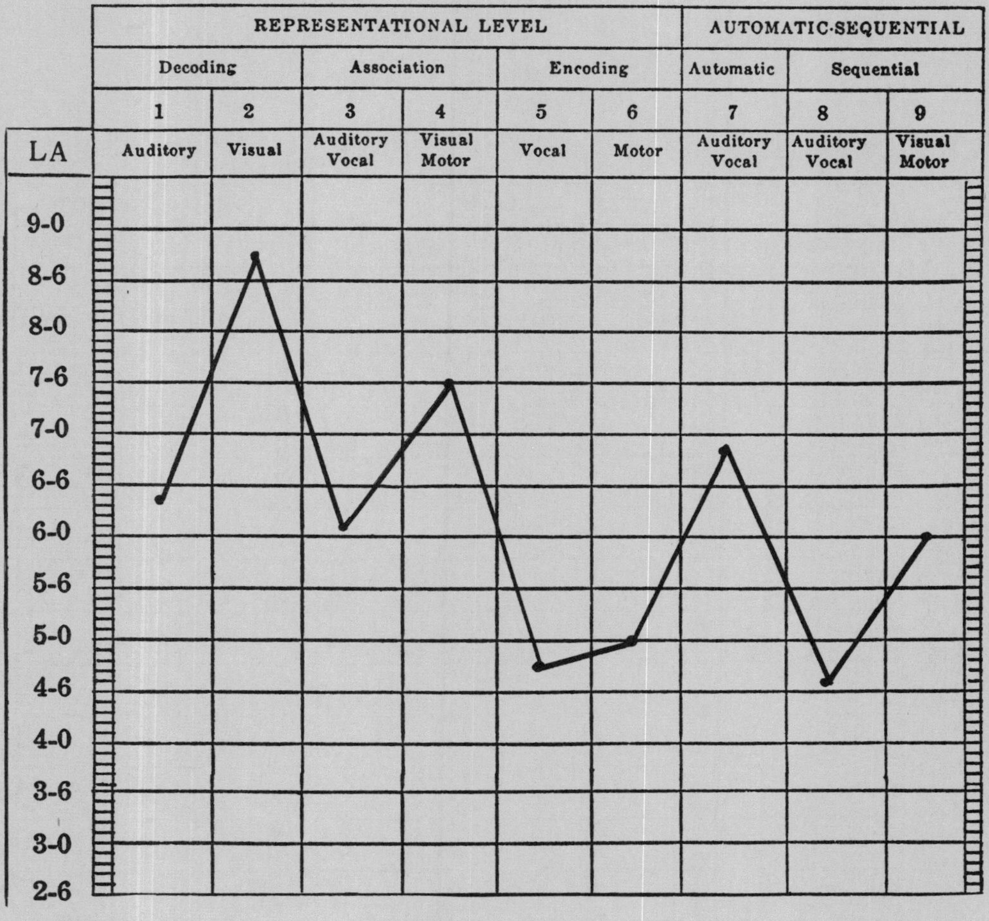

REPRESENTATIONAL LEVEL | AUTOMATIC-SEQUENTIAL

Decoding: 1 Auditory, 2 Visual | Association: 3 Auditory Vocal, 4 Visual Motor | Encoding: 5 Vocal, 6 Motor | Automatic: 7 Auditory Vocal | Sequential: 8 Auditory Vocal, 9 Visual Motor

LA: 9-0, 8-6, 8-0, 7-6, 7-0, 6-6, 6-0, 5-6, 5-0, 4-6, 4-0, 3-6, 3-0, 2-6

Additional Information

a. He appears to come from a very good home, achievement oriented, and full of pressure. If this is not the case, we then have a youngster with potentially extremely high intelligence but currently hampered by what would in fact constitute a severe auditory-vocal channel problem. The expressive problem is either the result of pressure in the home or the channel problem, but cannot tell which on the basis of the ITPA. In either case, he is currently operating in such a way that he is quite appropriately considered as having a learning disability although he is perhaps of quite high intelligence.

b. Definite auditory-vocal channel problem plus encoding difficulties. Bright youngster from a good home. Perhaps has been pressured by "pushy" parents.

FIGURE 36

Y. Q.

	REPRESENTATIONAL LEVEL						AUTOMATIC-SEQUENTIAL		
	Decoding		Association		Encoding		Automatic	Sequential	
	1	2	3	4	5	6	7	8	9
LA	Auditory	Visual	Auditory Vocal	Visual Motor	Vocal	Motor	Auditory Vocal	Auditory Vocal	Visual Motor
9-0									
8-6									
8-0									
7-6									
7-0									
6-6									
6-0									
5-6									
5-0									
4-6									
4-0									
3-6									
3-0									
2-6									

Additional Information

a. Appears mentally retarded; no learning disabilities evident.

b. Definitely appears to be borderline slow-learner or EMH. No learning problems beyond those expected.

FIGURE 37

D. R.

	REPRESENTATIONAL LEVEL						AUTOMATIC-SEQUENTIAL		
	Decoding		Association		Encoding		Automatic	Sequential	
	1	2	3	4	5	6	7	8	9
LA	Auditory	Visual	Auditory Vocal	Visual Motor	Vocal	Motor	Auditory Vocal	Auditory Vocal	Visual Motor
9-0									
8-6									
8-0									
7-6									
7-0									
6-6									
6-0									
5-6									
5-0									
4-6									
4-0									
3-6									
3-0									
2-6									

Additional Information

a. Somewhat of a slow learner. No gross learning problems noted. Prognosis for reading quite poor on the basis of low auditory memory.

b. Slow learner, slight predictable preference for visual channel. No real learning problems but reading prognosis doesn't look too bright.

FIGURE 38

B. S.

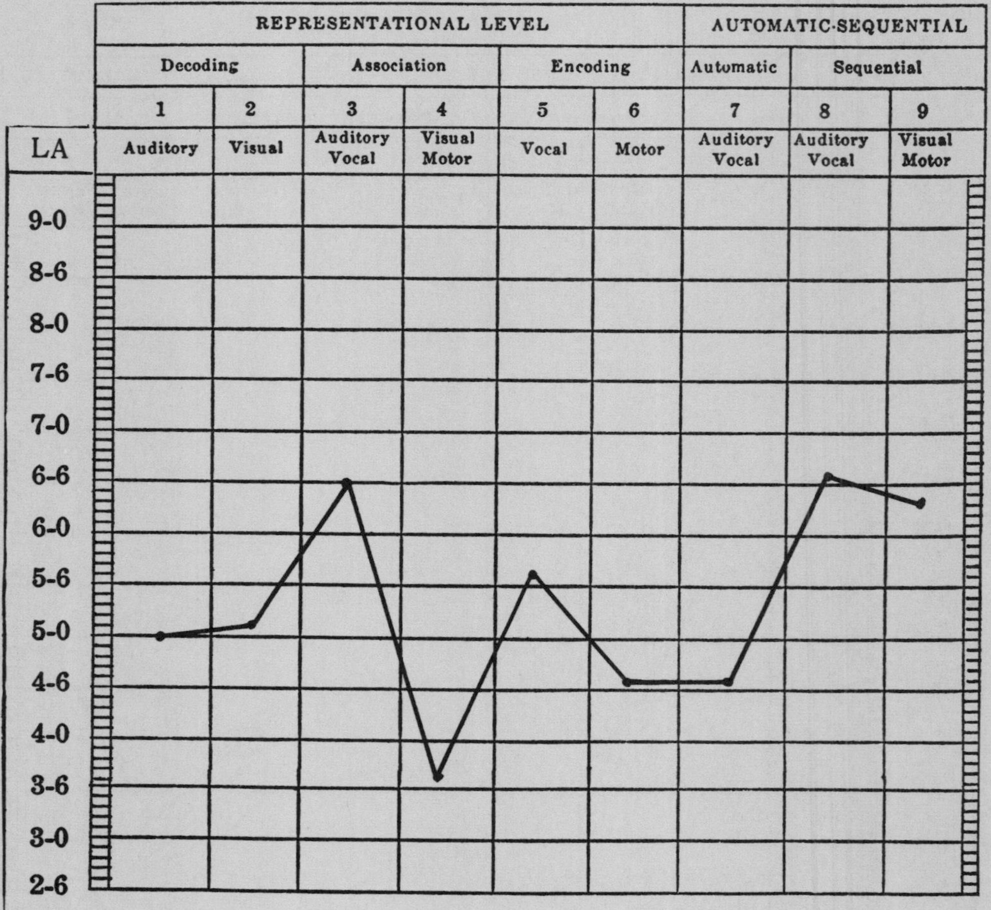

	REPRESENTATIONAL LEVEL						AUTOMATIC-SEQUENTIAL		
	Decoding		Association		Encoding		Automatic	Sequential	
	1	2	3	4	5	6	7	8	9
LA	Auditory	Visual	Auditory Vocal	Visual Motor	Vocal	Motor	Auditory Vocal	Auditory Vocal	Visual Motor
9-0									
8-6									
8-0									
7-6									
7-0									
6-6									
6-0									
5-6									
5-0									
4-6									
4-0									
3-6									
3-0									
2-6									

Additional Information

a. Very inconsistent profile. If intelligence is average he looks like a good prospect for reading. The discrepancy between auditory-vocal association and auditory-vocal automatic is unusual. Suggests difficulties in test administration. Other possibility is a very bright child from a poor home.

b. Somewhat strange profile. Would have to guess he is a fairly bright, non-conforming boy. Excellent memory. Low auditory vocal automatic is strange. Could be a poor home?

FIGURE 39

M. W.

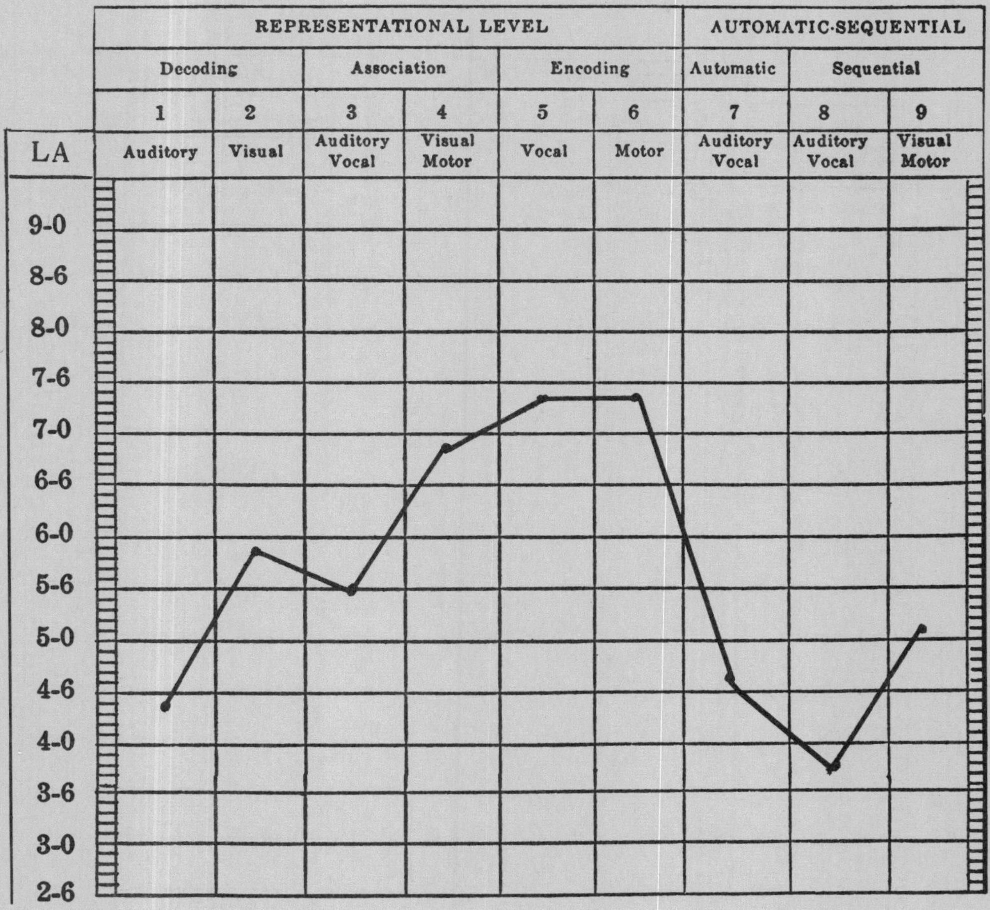

	REPRESENTATIONAL LEVEL						AUTOMATIC-SEQUENTIAL		
	Decoding		Association		Encoding		Automatic	Sequential	
	1	2	3	4	5	6	7	8	9
LA	Auditory	Visual	Auditory Vocal	Visual Motor	Vocal	Motor	Auditory Vocal	Auditory Vocal	Visual Motor
9-0									
8-6									
8-0									
7-6									
7-0									
6-6									
6-0									
5-6									
5-0									
4-6									
4-0									
3-6									
3-0									
2-6									

Additional Information

a. Appears to be of slightly below average intelligence but one who seems much brighter than this because of her high expressive ability. Suggests that this child is one about whom the teacher might feel "has more than she shows" when in fact the opposite is true. Picture of slow learner or even possible EMH is strongly suggested by the low automatic-sequential level.

b. This little gal will frustrate teachers because she looks like she has much more than she really does. Superficial, but very high expressive abilities. The automatic-sequential level looks like EMH. Reading prognosis is poor.

FIGURE 40

D. S.

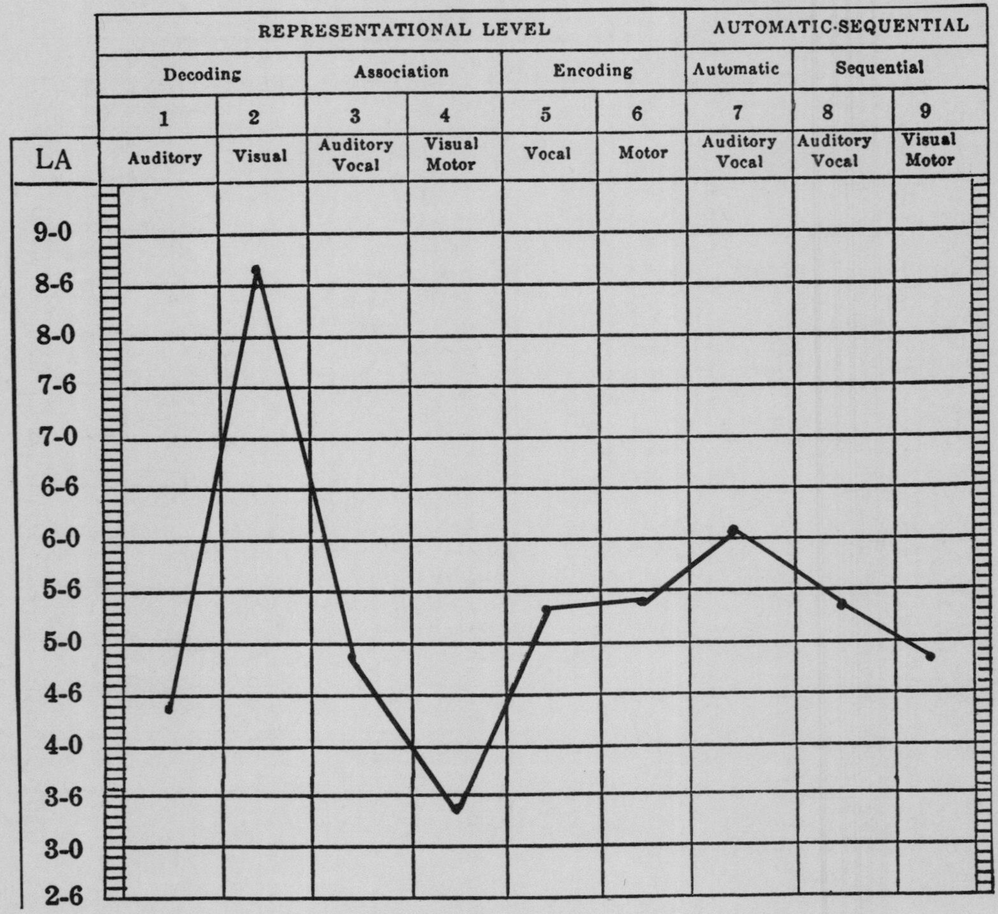

	REPRESENTATIONAL LEVEL						AUTOMATIC-SEQUENTIAL		
	Decoding		Association		Encoding		Automatic	Sequential	
	1	2	3	4	5	6	7	8	9
LA	Auditory	Visual	Auditory Vocal	Visual Motor	Vocal	Motor	Auditory Vocal	Auditory Vocal	Visual Motor

9-0
8-6
8-0
7-6
7-0
6-6
6-0
5-6
5-0
4-6
4-0
3-6
3-0
2-6

Additional Information

a. No learning disabilities evident. High visual decoding and low visual-motor association appear unreliable.

b. Large discrepancy between visual decoding and visual-motor association. Could be a fluke or could suggest slight emotional problems. Either extreme of compulsivity or deviant, far-out associations could account for this. No other learning problems are apparent. Both subtests should be checked.

FIGURE 41

B. S.

	REPRESENTATIONAL LEVEL						AUTOMATIC-SEQUENTIAL		
	Decoding		Association		Encoding		Automatic	Sequential	
	1	2	3	4	5	6	7	8	9
LA	Auditory	Visual	Auditory Vocal	Visual Motor	Vocal	Motor	Auditory Vocal	Auditory Vocal	Visual Motor
9-0									
8-6									
8-0									
7-6									
7-0									
6-6									
6-0									
5-6									
5-0									
4-6									
4-0									
3-6									
3-0									
2-6									

Additional Information

a. Mild Strauss syndrome or attentional problem. Fairly bright girl who is perhaps a creative or divergent youngster who does not work well with rote, sustained kinds of tasks. Auditory memory bears close watching. If it is confirmed as a memory-rather than distractibility problem, remediation would be in order.

b. Some suggestion of Strauss-type syndrome, especially poor attention span. Decoding also might need extra attention, although the visual decoding deficiency is part of the short attention span problem. Good home which encourages vocal expression, but perhaps is superficial. Can expect some trouble in reading.

FIGURE 42

J. J.

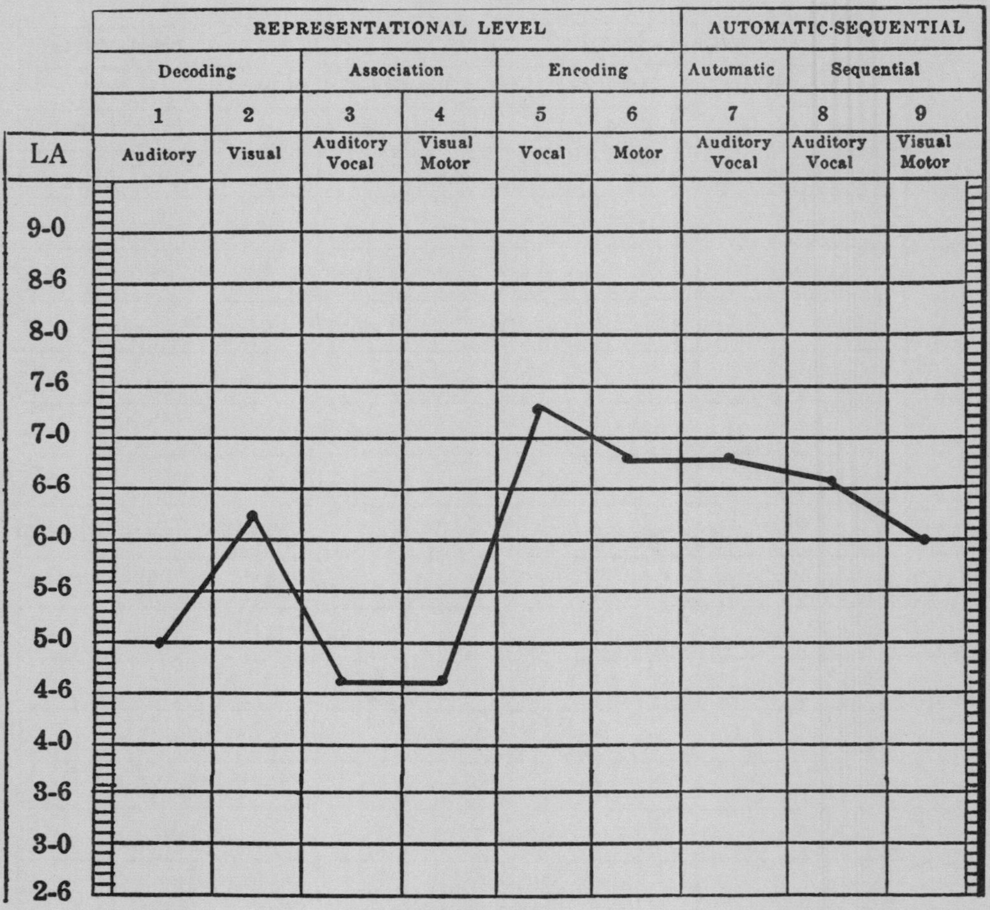

	REPRESENTATIONAL LEVEL						AUTOMATIC-SEQUENTIAL		
	Decoding		Association		Encoding		Automatic	Sequential	
	1	2	3	4	5	6	7	8	9
LA	Auditory	Visual	Auditory Vocal	Visual Motor	Vocal	Motor	Auditory Vocal	Auditory Vocal	Visual Motor

LA: 9-0, 8-6, 8-0, 7-6, 7-0, 6-6, 6-0, 5-6, 5-0, 4-6, 4-0, 3-6, 3-0, 2-6

Additional Information

a. Profile does not make much sense. Hard to see how both association areas can be down while the automatic-sequential level is up. Nevertheless would predict fairly good in reading, does not have severe learning disabilities as such unless the association deficit is genuine. If it is, concept formation-type remediation would be recommended.

b. Good home. Lots of encouragement. Perhaps even pressure. Should be a good bet for reading. Reasoning apparently weak. The preference for the automatic-sequential level is unusual and suggests rote learning comes more easily to him than do higher cognitive processes. Would guess association is badly in need of work. Might score as a slow learner on a verbal test.

CHAPTER 5

HANDLING ITPA DATA

Most ITPA users have occasion to compare and/or contrast two or more profiles or groups of profiles. The problem might be a fairly simple one involving only visual and subjective comparisons or it might be more complex, requiring some quantification of profiles. Frequently the question becomes one of how to reduce profiles to some "common denominator" so that differences in CA or MA can be controlled. The purpose of this section is to provide suggestions for possible ways to meaningfully and objectively compare profiles.

A first consideration in ITPA data treatment is that of what kind of subtest score to use--raw score, language age, or standard score. All have their uses, but at least two cautions should be kept in mind when selecting:

1. Standard scores have the disadvantages of (a) flattening profiles when the subjects' scores differ substantially from those of their CA peers; and (b) requiring four data card columns compared to two or rarely three for language ages (months).
2. The psycholinguistic age intervals between raw scores are unequal, and raw scores cannot be meaningfully plotted in relation to each other. Even change scores, computed in terms of raw scores, cannot be meaningfully compared across subtests.

For these reasons and others (see Bateman, 1967a), language ages are generally preferred by this writer. A word of caution is due, too, about the increasing use of total language age, especially in research projects. It is unequally weighted by certain subtests (e.g., auditory-vocal sequential contributes about twice as much as does motor encoding) and it in a real sense works at cross purposes to the entire philosophy of diagnosing specific abilities and disabilities.

Two related problems which often present themselves involve comparing and grouping profiles. One possible way to make meaningful comparisons without utilizing standard scores is to compute each subject's mean language age (the sum of his nine subtest language ages divided by nine) and record each subtest score in terms of months deviation from his own mean language age (LA). This procedure of utilizing LA as a reference line provides an objective way of operationally defining "discrepancy," "deficit," and "psycholinguistic disability" and enables the researcher to meaningfully combine and compare individual profiles and groups of profiles. A pilot study was conducted which found that the objective criterion of a ***total of subtest discrepancies from LA equal to 9 years*** corresponds to clinical judgment as constituting a case of "psycholinguistic disability." But further study suggested that the mean language age should be subtracted from the total discrepancy score to correct for increases in variability as a function of CA. If total discrepancy minus LA equals 3.5 to 4.0 years, a borderline disability is indicated. Differences greater than 4 years suggest a definite disability.

An additional use of LA and subtest deviation scores is suggested as an aid to grouping or matching profiles. When a child's subtest deviation scores are ranked in descending order his entire profile may then be coded at a glance. The coding system described below is a modification of Welsh's (1956) procedure for coding MMPI profiles.

A detailed example of the computation and coding of deviation scores is presented in Table 1 and the following discussion.

TABLE 1
Computation of Subtest Deviation Scores

Subtest No.	Raw Score	Language Age in Months	Deviation of Subtest from LA
7	7	51	-13 months
2	16	94	+30
6	17	88	+24
3	10	50	-14
9	0 (BN)	24*	-40
5	21	107	+43
8	4	30	-34
4	13	65	+ 1
1	21	71	+ 7
	Total =	580 months	206 months =
	LA =	64 months (580/9)	17.1 years

*Language ages below norms are arbitrarily assigned the value of 2-0 years, and the above norms scores are treated as 9-6 years.

Using the criterion of 9 years (108 months) total discrepancy as indicative of a psycholinguistic disability, it is clear that child A with a total discrepancy of 17.1 years (direction of deviation is ignored) has a disability. His highest performance was on subtest # 5 (+43 months), his next highest was on # 2 (+30 months) etc., and his lowest on # 9 (-40 months).

The subtest performances are ranked in descending order, so that his coded profile would read: 5 2 6 1 4 3 7 8 9. So far this tells us only the order, not the magnitude, of his performance on individual subtests in relation to his LA.

The following notations may be added to the coded profile above to indicate magnitude of deviation:

'' = 2 years or more above LA
* = Between 1 and 2 years above LA
(no notation) = Between 1 year above and 1 year below LA
/ = Between 1 and 2 years below LA
\# = 2 years or more below LA

The coded profile for child A now reads: 5'' 2'' 6* 1 4 3/ 7/ 8 #9 #.

This method of profile coding was used for the ITPAs of a group of 24 mentally retarded boys (CAs 7 to 10 years; IQs 42-84) as shown in Table 2. Data as shown in Table 2 can readily be analyzed by many nonparametric as well as informal procedures. A cursory glance at Table 2 reveals, e.g., that subtests 7, 8, and 9 appear more frequently than would be expected in the low performance positions. This relative weakness of retarded in the automatic-sequential level has been found in other studies (by much more laborious methods).

TABLE 2
Coded ITPA Profiles of 24 Retarded Boys

Subject No.									
1	9	1	3	4	2	6	5	8/	7/
2	1"	4*	5	3	2	6	7/	9/	8/
3	6*	2	5	4	9	3	8	1	7/
4	7"	1*	3	9	6	2/	4/	5/	8/
5	6"	5"	2	7	9	3	1	8/	4
6	5"	2"	6*	1	4	3/	7/	8	9
7	4*	3	9	5	1	8/	2/	6/	7
8	2"	6*	4	1	3	9	7/	5/	8
9	8"	5*	4	3	7	6	2/	1/	9/
10	8*	7*	3	4	2	6	9	1	5/
11	1"	2*	9*	6	5	4	3/	7/	8/
12	6*	2	3	7	9	5	1	4	8/
13	2*	1*	4	3	6	9	5	8/	7/
14	6*	2*	4	5	3	1	7	9/	8/
15	5*	1	2	4	6	9	3	7	8
16	4"	2"	6	5	7	1	9	3	8
17	1"	5*	9	2	3	8/	4/	6/	7/
18	1"	5*	7*	8	3	4/	9/	2/	6
19	5*	7*	3	8	2	1	4	9/	6
20	6"	2*	9*	1	4	3	7	5	8
21	1"	2	4	5	6	8	3	9	7/
22	5	8	1	6	3	2	4	7	9/
23	2"	4*	6	5	1	9	3/	7/	8/
24	4*	1*	3	9	2	6	5	8/	7

Attention is directed to subjects 15, 21, and 22. The coded notation in Table 2 reveals at a glance that these children had very even profiles with no suggestion of severe disabilities. On the other hand, subjects 6 and 20 show wide variations.

These observations are only suggestive of the many applications of the "coded deviation profile" to ITPA analysis.

Another possible technique for use both in grouping data and in interpreting individual profiles is that of converting subtest scores to quotients--language age divided by chronological age. This has much the same effect as standard scores, but is not subject to the levelling of standard scores, uses fewer data columns, and is more familiar to some. It is also a useful teaching technique for illustrating the concept of discrepancies among abilities. Figure 43 shows a youngster whose psycholinguistic quotients range from highly gifted in visual decoding and motor encoding (159, 144) to borderline in auditory memory (72).

Another technique potentially useful with the ITPA is that of correlating profiles with each other. This might have particular application to studies of the similarities and differences among siblings' and twins' profiles.

FIGURE 43

Profile Quotients

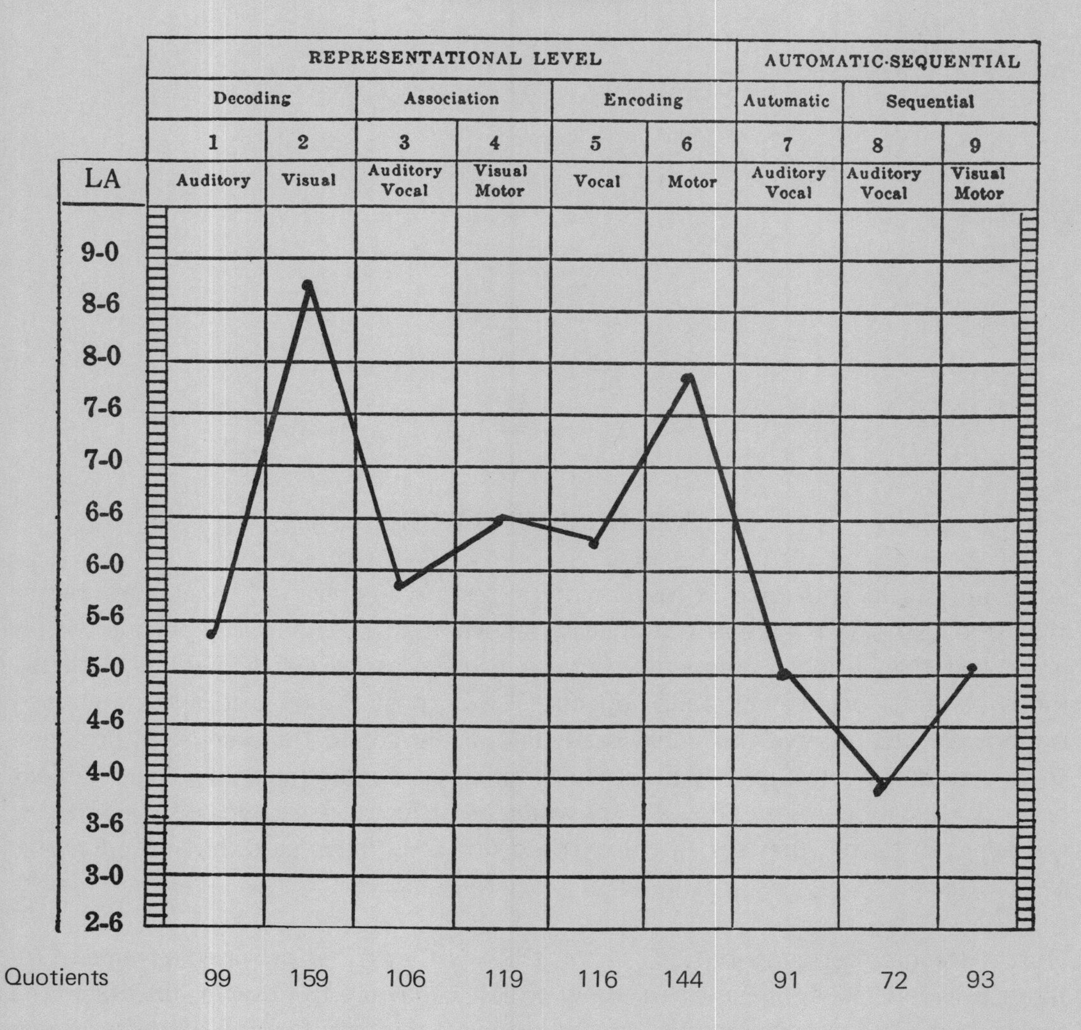

A CONCLUDING WORD

After all is said and done no psychological test, including the ITPA, is any better than the user. And there is nothing as important in developing expertise with a given test than using it frequently enough to become intimately familiar with the kinds of behaviors it elicits and reflects. The purpose of any test is to provide an opportunity to observe the behaviors believed relevant to the presenting problem. In one sense, the test is only an artificial gimmick standing between the examiner and the child's behavior. The ideal for which we strive is to learn to observe relevant behaviors so keenly that the test itself need not be administered, but only the profile plotted.

One of the greatest contributions of the ITPA is that it has provided a frame of reference which makes it easier to know which behaviors to observe, facilitates the observation, and provides guidelines for planning the modification of those behaviors through remediation.

REFERENCES

Bateman, Barbara D. A reference line for use with the Illinois Test of Psycholinguistic Abilities. J. SCH. PSYCH., 1967, 5, 128-35. (a)

Bateman, Barbara D. Reading: A controversial view. CURRICULUM BULLETIN: XXIII, No. 278. Eugene: Univer. of Oregon, School of Education, May, 1967 (b).

Bateman, Barbara D., and Wetherell, Janis. Psycholinguistic aspects of mental retardation. MENTAL RETARDATION, 3, April, 1965, 8-13.

Bateman, Barbara D. THE ILLINOIS TEST OF PSYCHOLINGUISTIC ABILITIES IN CURRENT RESEARCH: SUMMARIES OF STUDIES, Urbana, Ill.: Univer. of Illinois,Press, 1965.

Bateman, Barbara D. A comparison of two kindergartens. Unpublished data, Institute for Research on Exceptional Children, Univer. of Illinois, 1964.

Bateman, Barbara D. READING AND PSYCHOLINGUISTIC PROCESSES OF PARTIALLY SEEING CHILDREN. Washington, D. C.: Council for Exceptional Children Research Monographs, Series A, No. 5, 1963.

Ferrier, E. E. An investigation of the Illinois Test of Psycholinguistic Abilities performance of children with functional defects of articulation. EXCEPT. CHILD., 1966, 32, 625-629.

Foster, Suzanne. Language skills for children with persistent articulatory disorders. Unpublished doctoral dissertation, Texas Woman's Univer., 1963.

Kass, Corrine E. Psycholinguistic disabilities of children with reading problems. EXCEPT. CHILD., 1966, 32, 533-539.

Klaus, R. A. The Murfreesboro Project--Cognitive approaches to culturally disadvantaged children. SELECTED CONVENTION PAPERS, 43rd Annual CEC Convention. Washington, D. C.: Council for Exceptional Children, 1965, 249-255.

McCarthy, Jeanne McRae. Patterns of psycholinguistic development of mongoloid and non-mongoloid severely retarded children. AMER. J. MENT. DEFIC., (in press).

Mueller, M. W. Comparison of psycholinguistic patterns of gifted and retarded children. SELECTED CONVENTION PAPERS, 42nd Annual CEC Convention. Washington, D. C.: Council for Exceptional Children, 1964, 142-149.

Myers, Patricia. A study of language disabilities in cerebral palsied children. SPECH. & HRG. RES., 8, 1965, 129-136.

Olson, J. L. Deaf and sensory aphasic children. EXCEPT. CHILD., 1961, 27, 422-424.

Ragland, G. G. The performance of educable mentally handicapped students of differing reading ability on the ITPA. SELECTED CONVENTION PAPERS, 44th Annual CEC Convention, Washington, D. C.: Council for Exceptional Children, 1966, 69-72.

Reichstein, J. Auditory threshold consistency: a basic characteristic for differential diagnosis of children with communication disorders. Unpublished doctoral dissertation, Teacher's College, Columbia Univer., 1963.

Weaver, S. J. Psycholinguistic abilities of culturally deprived children. In EARLY TRAINING PROJECT, MURFREESBORO, TENN.: Tennessee City Schools and George Peabody College for Teachers, Nov., 1963.

Welsh, G. S. and Dahlstrom, W. (eds.). BASIC READINGS ON THE MMPI IN PSYCHOLOGY AND MEDICINE. Minneapolis: Univer. of Minnesota Press, 1956.

Wiseman, D. E. Program planning for retarded children with psycholinguistic disabilities. Unpublished doctoral dissertation. Univer. of Illinois, 1966.

APPENDIX

Bibliography of ITPA Literature 1960-1967

Compiled by Barbara Bateman

and

Andrea Pickman

I. BACKGROUND AND GENERAL REFERENCES

Kirk, S. A., & Bateman, Barbara. TEN YEARS OF RESEARCH. Urbana, Ill.: Institute for Research on Exceptional Children, Univer. of Ill., 1964.

McCarthy, J. J., & Kirk, S. A. ILLINOIS TEST OF PSYCHOLINGUISTIC ABILITIES, EXAMINER'S MANUAL. Urbana, Ill.: Univer. of Ill. Press, 1961.

Osgood, C. E. CONTEMPORARY APPROACHES TO COGNITION. Cambridge, Mass.: Harvard Univer. Press, 1957.

Osgood, C. E., & Miron, M. S. (eds.) APPROACHES TO THE STUDY OF APHASIA. Urbana, Ill.: Univer. of Ill. Press, 1963.

Wepman, J. M., Jones, L. V., Bock, R.D., & Pelt, D. V. Studies in aphasia: back- and theoretical formulations. J. SPEECH AND HEARING DISORDERS, 1960, 25, 323-332.

II. MONOGRAPHS AND CHAPTERS

Anderson, Gladys L. & Magary, J. F. Projective techniques and the Illinois test of Psycholinguistic Abilities, in SCHOOL PSYCHOLOGICAL SERVICES (ed., J. F. Magary.) Englewood Cliff, N. J.: Prentice-Hall, 1967.

Bateman, Barbara. An educator's view of a diagnostic approach to learning disorders. In LEARNING DISORDERS, Vol. I (ed., J. Hellmuth), Seattle, Wash.: Special Child Publications, 1965.

Bateman, Barbara. CLINICAL INTERPRETATION OF THE 1961 EXPERIMENTAL EDITION OF THE ILLINOIS TEST OF PSYCHOLINGUISTIC ABILITIES. Seattle, Wash.: Special Child Publications, in press.

Bateman, Barbara. Reading: A controversial view. CURRICULUM BULLETIN: XXIII, No. 278. Eugene, Ore.: Univer. of Oregon, School of Education, May, 1967.

Bateman, Barbara. READING AND PSYCHOLINGUISTIC PROCESSES OF PARTIALLY SEEING CHILDREN. Washington, D. C.: Council for Exceptional children Research Monographs, Series A, No. 5, 1963.

Bateman, Barbara. THE ILLINOIS TEST OF PSYCHOLINGUISTIC ABILITIES IN CURRENT RESEARCH: SUMMARIES OF STUDIES, Urbana, Ill.: Univer. of Illinois Press, 1965.

Karnes, Merle; Hodgins, Audrey, et. al. ACTIVITIES FOR DEVELOPING PSYCHOLINGUISTIC SKILLS WITH PRESCHOOL CULTURALLY DISADVANTAGED CHILDREN. Urbana, Ill.: Institute for Research on Exceptional Children, University of Ill., 1966.

Kirk, S. A. Amelioration of mental disabilities through psychodiagnostic and remedial procedures. In MENTAL RETARDATION, (ed., G. A. Jervis) Springfield, Ill.: Charles C. Thomas, 1967.

Kirk, S. A. THE DIAGNOSIS AND REMEDIATION OF PSYCHOLINGUISTIC DISABILITIES. Urbana, Ill.: Institute for Research on Exceptional Children, Univer. of Ill., 1966.

Kirk, S. A. The Illinois Test of Psycholinguistic Abilities: Its origin and implications. In LEARNING DISORDERS, Vol. 3, (ed., J. Hellmuth) Seattle: Special Child Publications, in press.

McCarthy, J. J., & Kirk, S. A. THE CONSTRUCTION, STANDARDIZATION AND STATISTICAL CHARACTERISTICS OF THE ILLINOIS TEST OF PSYCHOLINGUISTIC ABILITIES. Urbana, Ill.: Univer. of Ill. Press, 1963.

McCarthy, J. J., & Olson, J. L. VALIDITY STUDIES ON THE ILLINOIS TEST OF PSYCHOLINGUISTIC ABILITIES. Urbana, Ill.: Univer. of Ill. Press, 1964.

Sievers, Dorothy J., McCarthy, J. J., Olson, J. L., Bateman, Barbara D., & Kass, Corrine E. SELECTED STUDIES ON THE ILLINOIS TEST OF PSYCHOLINGUISTIC ABILITIES. Urbana, Ill.: Univers of Ill. Press, 1963.

Smith, J. O. Effects of group language development program upon the psycholinguistic abilities of educable mental retardates. Nashville, Tenn.: SPECIAL EDUCATION RES. MONOGR., No. 1, George Peabody College, 1962.

III. ARTICLES AND PAPERS

Altonen, Anita Louise. Classroom techniques: Language training for the mentally retarded. EDUC. AND TRNG. OF THE MENTALLY RETARDED, 1967, 2, 70-74.

Bateman, Barbara D. A pilot study of mentally retarded children attending summer day camp. MENTAL RETARDATION, (in press, available from author).

Bateman, Barbara D. A reference line for use with the Illinois Test of Psycholinguistic Abilities. J. SCH. PSYCH., 5, 1967, 128-135.

Bateman, Barbara D. Learning disabilities--an overview. J. SCH. PSYCH., 3, 1965, 1-12.

Bateman, Barbara D. Learning disabilities, -- yesterday, today, and tomorrow. EXCEPT. CHILD., 31, 1964, 166-167.

Bateman, Barbara D. Mild visual defects and learning problems in partially seeing children. SIGHT-SAVING REVIEW, 1963, 33, 30-33.

Bateman, Barbara D. The application of language and communication models in programs for the trainable retarded. SELECTED CONVENTION PAPERS, 44th Annual CEC Convention. Washington, D. C.: Council for Exceptional Children, 1966, 45-49.

Bateman, Barbara D. The role of the Illinois Test of Psycholinguistic Abilities in differential diagnosis and program planning for mentally retarded. AMER. J. ORTHOPSYCH., 1965, 35, 465-472.

Bateman, Barbara D., & Wetherell, Janis. Psycholinguistic aspects of mental retardation. MENTAL RETARDATION, 3, 1965, 8-13.

Bilovsky, D. & Share, J. The Illinois Test of Psycholinguistic Abilities and Down's syndrome: An exploratory study. AMER. J. MENT. DEFIC., 1965, 70, 78-82.

Blessing, K. R. Remediation of psycholinguistic deficits in retarded children. BUREAU MEMORANDUM 6, (4): 20-29, 1965. Reprint issued from Bureau for Handicapped Children, State Dept. of Public Instruction, Madison, Wisc.

Blue, C. M. The effectiveness of a group language program with trainable mental retardates. Unpublished report, Appalachian State Teachers College, Boone, North Carolina, 1963.

Bradley, Betty H., Maurer, Ruth, & Hundziak, Marcel. A study of the effectiveness of milieu therapy and language training for the mentally retarded. EXCEPT. CHILD., 33, 1966, 143-150.

Brown, L. F. & Rice, J. A. Psycholinguistic differentiation of low IQ children. MENTAL RETARDATION, 5, 1967, 16-20.

Chang, T. C. A study of language abilities. HAWAII SCHOOLS, Vol. 2, No. 2, Oct. 1964, 4-5. (Hawaii State Dept. of Educ., Honolulu).

Cripe, Antje E. Auditory and visual learning related to Illinois Test of Psycholinguistic Abilities sensory channels. SELECTED CONVENTION PAPERS, 44th Annual CEC Convention. Washington, D. C.: Council for Exceptional Children, 1966, 152-154.

Ensminger, E. E. & Smith, J. O. Language development and the Illinois Test of Psycholinguistic Abilities. THE TRAINING SCHOOL BULLETIN, 1965, 62, 97-107.

Ferrier, E. E. An investigation of the Illinois Test of Psycholinguistic Abilities performance of children with functional defects of articulation. EXCEPT. CHILD., 1966, 32, 625-629.

Gunzburg, H. C. The reliability of a test of psycholinguistic abilities. (I. T. P. A.) in a population of young male subnormals. J. OF MENT. SUBNORMALITY, 10, 1964, 101-112.

Harries, W. T. The Illinois Test of Psycholinguistic Abilities (ITPA): An appraisal. Australian Council for Educational Research, MEMO No., 1, Jan., 1965.

Hart, N. W. M. The differential diagnosis of the psycholinguistic abilities of the cerebral palsied child and effective remedial procedures. SPECIAL SCHOOLS BULLETIN, No. 2, Brisbane, Australia, 1963.

Hasterok, G. S. The training of mentally retarded children with sense modality disabilities. SELECTED CONVENTION PAPERS, 42nd Annual CEC Convention, Washington, D. C.: Council for Exceptional Children, 1964, 128-131.

Hirsch, Esther. Training of visualizing ability by the kinesthetic method of teaching reading. SELECTED CONVENTION PAPERS, 42nd Annual CEC Convention, Washington, D. C.: Council for Exceptional Children, 1964, 131-139.

Kass, Corrine E. Psycholinguistic disabilities of children with reading problems. EXCEPT. CHILD., 1966, 32, 533-539.

Kenney, Eleanore T. The small classroom--a developmental idiosyncratic approach to learning and behavioral disorders in children of normal intelligence. SELECTED CONVENTION PAPERS. 42nd Annual CEC Convention. Washington, D. C.: Council for Exceptional Children, 1964, 208-216.

Kirk, S. A. & Bateman, Barbara. Diagnosis and remediation of learning diabilities. EXCEPT. CHILD., 1962, 29, 73-78. Also in SELECTED CONVENTION PAPERS, 40th Annual CEC Convention, Washington, D. C.: Council for Exceptional Children, 1962, 99-102.

Kirk, S. A., & McCarthy, J. J. The Illinois Test of Psycholinguistic Abilities--an approach to differential diagnosis. AMER. J. MENT. DEFIC., 1961, 66, 399-412.

Kirk, S. A.; McLeod, J. Research studies in psycholinguistic disabilities. SELECTED CONVENTION PAPERS, 44th Annual CEC Convention, Washington, D. C.: Council for Exceptional Children, 1966, 173-184.

Klaus, R. A. The Murfreesboro Project--Cognitive approaches to culturally disadvantaged children. SELECTED CONVENTION PAPERS, 43rd Annual CEC Convention. Washington, D. C.: Council for Exceptional Children, 1965, 249-255.

Larson, R. & Olson, J. L. A method of identifying culturally deprived kindergarten children. EXCEPT. CHILD. 30, 1963, 131-134.

Loeffler, F. J. An extension and partial replication of Meyers, et al.'s primary abilities at mental age six. Paper presented at the biennial meeting of the Society for Research in Child Development, Berkeley, Calif., April, 1963.

McCarthy, J. J. Notes on the validity of the ITPA. MENTAL RETARDATION, 1965, 3, 25-26.

McCarthy, J. J. The importance of linguistic ability in the mentally retarded. MENTAL RETARDATION, 1964, 2, 90-95.

McCarthy, J. J. A response, EXCEPT. CHILD., 1967, 33, 380-381.

McCarthy, J. J. The use and usefulness of the Illinois Test of Psycholinguistic Abilities. SELECTED CONVENTION PAPERS, 42nd Annual CEC Convention. Washington, D. C.: Council for Exceptional Children, 1964, 195-201.

McCarthy, Jeanne McRae. Patterns of psycholinguistic development of mongoloid and non-mongoloid severely retarded children. AMER. J. MENT. DEFIC., (in press).

McLeod, J. Dyslexia in young children and A factorial study, with special reference to the Illinois Test of Psycholinguistic Abilities. Urbana, Ill.: Institute for Research on Exceptional Children, Univer. of Illinois, 1967. Mimeo.

Mueller, M. W. Comparison of psycholinguistic patterns of gifted and retarded children. J. SCH. PSYCH., 1965, 3, 18-26. (Also in SELECTED CONVENTION PAPERS, 42nd Annual CEC Convention, Washington, D. C.: Council for Exceptional Children, 1964, 143-148).

Mueller, M. W. Language profiles of mentally retarded children. SELECTED CONVENTION PAPERS, 42nd Annual CEC Convention, Washington, D. C.: Council for Exceptional Children, 1964, 149-153.

Mueller, M. W. Peabody College Research on the Illinois Test of Psycholinguistic Abilities. SELECTED CONVENTION PAPERS, 41st Annual CEC Convention. Washington, D. C.: Council for Exceptional Children, 1963, 183-187.

Mueller, M. W., & Smith, J. O. The stability of language age modifications over time. AMER. J. MENT. DEFIC., 1964, 68, 537-539.

Mueller, M. W., & Weaver, S. J. Psycholinguistic abilities of institutionalized and non-institutionalized trainable mental retardates. Amer. J. Ment. Defic., 1964, 68, 775-783. (study reviewed in Mueller, M. W., Peabody College Abilities, SELECTED CONVENTION PAPERS, 41st Annual CEC Convention. Washington, D. C.: Council for Exceptional Children, 1963, 183-187.)

Myers, Patricia. A study of language disabilities in cerebral palsied children. SPCH. & HRG. RES., 8, 1965, 129-136.

Olson, J. L. Deaf and sensory aphasic children. EXCEPT. CHILD., 1961, 27, 422-424.

Olson, J. L.; Hahn, H. R. & Herman, Anita. Psycholinguistic curriculum, MENTAL RETARDATION, 1965, 3, 14-19.

Outridge, M. Psycholinguistic abilities of five children attending a Brisbane Opportunity School. THE SLOW LEARNING CHILD, 1965, 2, 165-176.

Painter, Genevieve B. The effect of a rhythmic and sensory-motor activity program on perceptual-motor-spatial abilities of kindergarten children. EXCEPT. CHILD., 1966, 33, 113-116.

Ragland, G. G. The performance of educable mentally handicapped students of differing reading ability on the Illinois Test of Psycholinguistic Abilities. Selected Convention Papers, 44th Annual CEC Convention, Washington, D. C., Council for Exceptional Children, 1966, 69-72.

Reichstein, J. Auditory threshold consistency indifferential diagnosis of aphasia in children. J. SPCH. & HRG. DIS., 1964, 29, 147-155.

Roseberg, M. B. A coordinated approach to correction of learning disabilities in Public School children, in Educational Therapy, Vol. 1, (ed. J. Hellmuth) in Seattle: Special Child Publications, 1966.

Rychman, D. B. A comparison of information processing abilities of middle and lower class Negro kindergarten boys. EXCEPT. CHILD., 33, 1967, 545-550.

Semmel, M. I., & Mueller, M. W. A factor analysis of the Illinois Test of Psycholinguistic Abilities with mentally retarded children. Unpublished study, Geo. Peabody College, 1962. (Study reviewed in Mueller, M. W., Peabody College Research on the Illinois Test of Psycholinguistic Abilities, SELECTED CONVENTION PAPERS, 41st Annual CEC Convention, Washington, D. C.: Council for Exceptional children, 1963, 183-187).

Sheperd, G. Selected factors in the reading ability of educable mentally retarded boys. AMER. J. MENT. DEFIC., 71, 1967, 563-570.

Smith, J. O. Group language development for educable mental retardates. EXCEPT. CHILD., 1962, 29, 95-101.

Spicker, H. H. Research implications: The remediation of language deficiencies of educable mentally retarded children. EDUC. AND TRNG. OF THE MENT. RETARD., 1966, 1, 137-140.

Spicker, H. H.; Hodges, W. L., & McCandless. A diagnostically based curriculum for psychosocially deprived preschool mentally retarded children: Interim report. EXCEPT. CHILD., 1966, 33, 215-220.

Stark, J. Performance of aphasic children on the Illinois Test of Psycholinguistic Abilities. EXCEPT. CHILD., 1966, 33, 153-160.

Tubbs, Virginia K. Types of linguistic disability in psychotic children. J. MENT. DEFIC. RES., 1966, 10, 230-240.

Weener, P.; Barritt, L. S., & Semmel, M. I. Forum: A critical evaluation of the Illinois Test of Psycholinguistic abilities. EXCEPT. CHILD., 1967, 33, 373-379.

Weener, P; Barritt, L. S. & Semmel, M. I. A reply to McCarthy. EXCEPT. CHILD., 1967, 33, 382-386.

Wiseman, D. E. A classroom procedure for identifying and remediating language problems. MENTAL RETARDATION, 1965, 3, 20-24.

Wiseman, D. E. Program planning for retarded children with psycholinguistic abilities. SELECTED CONVENTION PAPERS, 42nd Annual CEC Convention, Washington, D. C.: Council for Exceptional Children, 1964, 241-252.

IV. RESEARCH REPORTS -- FINAL AND IN PROGRESS

Bateman, Barbara. Project Camping - 1965: Preliminary report of a study of mentally retarded children attending summer day camp. Mimeo. (Report submitted to the Jos. P. Kennedy, Jr. Foundation), 1965.

Bateman, Barbara. Project Camping - 1965: Selected data analysis continuation. Mimeo., (Report submitted to Jos. P. Kennedy, Jr. Foundation), 1965.

Beadle, Kathryn R. Prevention and early detection of learning disabilities and language disorders in a culturally deprived program. Head Start Language Research Program Final Report, State of Hawaii, Dept. of Educ., General Educ. Branch, Kindergarten-Primary Educ. Section, Honolulu, Hawaii 96804.

Beery, K. E. Preschool prediction and prevention of learning disabilities. Final Report, 1967, Project Nos. 6-8742 & 6-8743, Grant Nos. OEG 4-7-008742-2031 & OEG 4-7-008743-1507, Office of Educ., U. S. Dept. of HEW.

Deutsch, Cynthia P. Patterns of perceptual, language, and intellective performance in children with cognitive deficits. (Tenth Quarter Progress Report 9/1/66 - 11/30/66) Institute for Developmental Studies, New York University, School of Education, Washington Square, New York, N. Y. 10003.

Ensminger, E. E. The effects of a classroom language development program on psycholinguistic abilities and intellectual functioning in culturally deprived, slow learning children. Unpubl. Working Paper, Special Educ., Univer. of Kansas, 1965.

Goldstein, H.; Moss, J. W., & Jordan, Laura. The efficacy of special class training on the development of mentally retarded children, Cooperative Research Project No. 610. U. S. Dept. of HEW, 1965. (See especially Appendix C, The psycholinguistic abilities of children whose IQ's are below average, Barbara D. Bateman, 183-197.

Gray, Susan W., Weaver, Ann, & Starke, Christiane. Language abilities in the children of the Early Training Project. (Abstract). In: ABSTRACTS OF PEABODY STUDIES IN MENTAL RETARDATION 1962-1964. 3 (-): Abstract No. 58, 1965.

Hall, E. P. Language retardation detection and prevention follow through, 1966 Summer Project. Final Report, State of Hawaii, Dept. of Educ., General Educ. Branch, Kindergarten-Primary Section, Honolulu, Hawaii 96804.

Mueller, N. W. & Dunn, L. M. A classroom language development program for educable mental retardates. Unpubl. working paper # 2, Geo. Peabody College for Teachers, 1964.

Painter, Genevieve. Psychological analysis of camp activities in selected Kennedy Foundation sponsored camps for the mentally retarded. IREC, Univer. of Ill. (Report submitted to Jos. P. Kennedy, Jr. Foundation), 1965.

Pennsylvania, Commonwealth of. Preschool and primary education project-1965-66 Annual progress report; Harrisburg, 1967. Dept. of Public Instruction, Public Welfare and Health.

Strong, R. T., Jr. Multidimensional studies of psycholinguistic abilities in neurologically impaired mentally retarded children. Unpublished progress report, Grant No. R-162-63. United Cerebral Palsy Research and Educational Foundation, 1963.

Weaver, S. J. Psycholinguistic abilities of culturally deprived children. In EARLY TRAINING PROJECT, MURFREESBORO, TENN.: Tennessee City Schools and George Peabody College for Teachers, Nov. 1963.

V. UNPUBLISHED THESES & DISSERTATIONS

Blessing, K. R. An investigation of a psycholinguistic deficit in educable mentally retarded children: detection, remediation and related variables. Unpublished doctoral dissertation, Univer. of Wisc., 1964.

Center, W. R. A factor analysis of three language and communication batteries. Unpublished doctoral dissertation, Univer. of Georgia, 1963.

Dillon, E. J. An investigation of basic psycholinguistic and reading abilities among the cerebral palsied. Unpublished doctoral dissertation, Temple Univer., 1966.

Egeland, B. R. The relationship of intelligence, visual-motor skills and psycholinguistic abilities with achievement in the first grade. Unpublished doctoral dissertation, Univer. of Iowa, 1966.

Espeseth, K. V. Effect of a three month training program to improve visual sequencing ability in deaf children. Unpublished doctoral dissertation, Univer. of Wisc., 1964.

Foster, Suzanne. Language skills for children with persistent articulatory disorders. Unpublished doctoral dissertation, Texas Women's Univer., 1963.

Hermann, Anita. An experimental approach to the educability of psycholinguistic functions in children. Unpublished master's thesis, Univer. of Ill., 1962.

Horner, R. D. A factor analysis comparison of the ITPA and PLS with mentally retarded children. Kansas State College of Pittsburg. Unpublished master's thesis. 1967.

Hurley, O. L. The interrelationships of intersensory integration, visual sequential memory, spatial ability, and reading ability in second and third graders. Unpublished doctoral dissertation, Univer. of Ill., 1965.

Stearns, K. P. Experimental group language development for psycho-socially deprived preschool children. Unpublished doctoral dissertation, Indiana Univer., 1966.

Strunk, D. K., II. An analysis of the psycholinguistic abilities of a selected group of mongoloids. Unpublished doctoral dissertation, Univer. of Va., 1964.

Sutton, Peggy R. The relationship of visualizing ability to reading. Unpublished master's thesis, Univer. of Ill., 1963.

Weld, R. G. An investigation of the long term effects of language training in the mentally retarded. Unpublished master's thesis, Univer. of Wisc., 1964.

Wetherell, Janis Lynne. Auditory memory, Unpublished bachelor's thesis, Univer. of Ill., 1964.

Wiseman, D. E. The effects of an individualized remedial program or mentally retarded children with psycholinguistic disabilities. Unpublished doctoral dissertation, Univer. of Illinois, 1965.

The following doctoral dissertations have been published and referrals to the published material have been cited above.

Bateman, Barbara. Reading and psycholinguistic processes of partially sighted children. Univer. of Ill., 1962.

Ferrier, E. E. An investigation of psycholinguistic factors associated with functional defects of articulation. Univer. of Ill., 1963.

Hasterok, G. S. The learning performance of retarded children with visual and auditory sense modality disabilities. Univer. of Ill., 1964.

Hirsch, Esther. Training of visualizing ability by the Kinesthetic method of teaching reading. Unpublished master's thesis, Univer. of Ill., 1963.

Kass, Corrine E. Some psychological correlates of severe reading disability. Univer. of Ill., 1962.

McCarthy, Jeanne M. Patterns of psycholinguistic development of mongoloid and non-mongoloid severely retarded children. Univer. of Ill., 1965.

Myers, Patricia. A comparison of language disabilities of young spastic and athetoid children. Univer. of Texas, 1963.

Olson, J. L. A comparison of receptive aphasic, expressive aphasic, and deaf children on the Illinois Test of Psycholinguistic abilities. Univer. of Ill., 1960.

Painter, Genevieve B. The effect of a rhythmic and sensory-motor activity program on perceptual-motor-spatial abilities of kindergarten children. Unpublished master's thesis, Univer. of Ill., 1964.

Ragland, G. G. The performance of educable mentally handicapped students of differing reading ability on the ITPA. Univer. of Va., 1964.

Reichstein, J. Auditory threshold consistency: a basic characteristic for differential diagnosis of children with communication disorders. Teacher's College, Columbia Univer., 1963.

Ryckman, D. B. Psychological processes of disadvantaged children. Univer. of Ill., 1966.